AN ESSAY ON CRIMES AND PUNISHMENTS

WITH A COMMENTARY BY M. DE VOLTAIRE.

CESARE BECCARIA

CONTENTS

A COMMENTARY ON THE BOOK OF CRIMES AND PUNISHMENTS.

PREFACE OF THE TRANSLATOR.

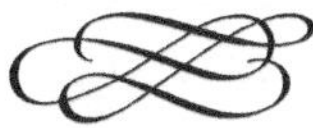

PENAL LAWS, so considerable a part of every system of legislation, and of so great importance to the happiness, peace and security of every member of society, are still so imperfect, and are attended with so many unnecessary circumstances of cruelty in all nations, that an attempt to reduce them to the standard of reason must be interesting to all mankind. It is not surprising then, that this little book hath engaged the attention of all ranks of people in every part of Europe. It is now about eighteen months since the first publication; in which time it hath passed no less than six editions in the original language; the third of which was printed within six months after its first appearance. It hath been translated into French; that translation hath also been several times reprinted, and perhaps no book, on any subject, was ever received with more avidity, more generally read, or more universally applauded.

The author is the Marquis BECCARIA, of Milan. Upon considering the nature of the religion and government under which he lives, the reasons for concealing his name are obvious. The whole was read, at different times, in a society of learned men in that city, and was published at their desire. As to the translation, I have preserved the order of the original, except in a paragraph or two, which I have taken the liberty to restore to the chapters to which they evidently belong, and from which they must have been accidentally detached. The French translator hath gone much farther; he hath not only transposed every chapter, but every paragraph in the whole book. But in this, I conceive he hath assumed a right which belongs not to any translator, and which cannot be justified. His disposition may appear more systematical, but certainly the author has as undoubted a right to the arrangement of his own ideas as to the ideas themselves; and therefore to destroy that arrangement, is to pervert his meaning, if he had any meaning in his plan, the contrary to which can hardly be supposed.

With regard to the Commentary, attributed to Mons. de Voltaire, my only authority for supposing it his, is the voice of the public, which indeed is the only authority we have for most of his works. Let those who are acquainted with the peculiarity of his manner judge for themselves.

The facts above mentioned would preclude all apology for this translation, if any apology were necessary, for translating into our language a work, which, from the nature of the subject, must be interesting to every nation; but must be particularly acceptable to the English, from the eloquent and forcible manner in which the author pleads the cause of liberty, benevolence and humanity. It may however be objected, that a treatise of this kind is useless in England, where, from the excellence of our laws and government, no examples of cruelty or oppression are to be found. But it must also be allowed, that much is still wanting to perfect our system of legislation; the confinement of debtors, the filth and horror of our prisons, the cruelty of jailors, and the extortion of the petty officers of justice, to all which may be added the melancholy reflection, that the number of criminals put to death in England is much greater than in any other part of Europe, are considerations which will sufficiently answer every objection. These are my only reasons for endeavouring to diffuse the knowledge of the useful truths contained in this little essay; and I say, with my author, that if I can be instrumental in rescuing a single victim from the hand of tyranny or ignorance, his transports will sufficiently console me for the contempt of all mankind.

INTRODUCTION

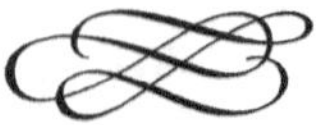

I N every human society, there is an effort continually tending to confer on one part the height of power and happiness, and to reduce the other to the extreme of weakness and misery. The intent of good laws is to oppose this effort, and to diffuse their influence universally and equally. But men generally abandon the care of their most important concerns to the uncertain prudence and discretion of those, whose interest it is to reject the best and wisest institutions; and it is not till they have been led into a thousand mistakes, in matters the most essential to their lives and liberties, and are weary of suffering, that they can be induced to apply a remedy to the evils with which they are oppressed. It is then they begin to conceive, and acknowledge the most palpable truths, which, from their very simplicity, commonly escape vulgar minds, incapable of analysing objects, accustomed to receive impressions without distinction, and to be determined rather by the opinions of others, than by the result of their own examination.

If we look into history we shall find that laws which are, or ought to be, conventions between men in a state of freedom, have been, for the most part, the work of the passions of a few, or the consequences of a fortuitous or temporary necessity; not dictated by a cool examiner of human nature, who knew how to collect in one point the actions of a multitude, and had this only end in view, *the greatest happiness of the greatest number.* Happy are those few nations who have not waited till the slow succession of human vicissitudes should, from the extremity of evil, produce a transition to good; but, by prudent laws, have facilitated the progress from one to the other! And how great are the obligations due from mankind to that philosopher, who, from the obscurity of his closet, had the courage to scatter among the multitude the seeds of useful truths, so long unfruitful!

The art of printing has diffused the knowledge of those philosophical truths, by which the relations between sovereigns and their subjects, and between nations, are discovered. By this knowledge commerce is animated, and there has sprung up a spirit of emulation and industry worthy of rational beings. These are the produce of this enlightened age; but the cruelty of punishments, and the irregularity of proceeding in criminal cases, so principal a part of the legislation, and so much neglected throughout Europe, has hardly ever been called in question. Errors, accumulated through many centuries, have never been exposed by ascending to general principles; nor has the force of acknowledged truths been ever opposed to the unbounded licentiousness of ill-directed power, which has continually produced so many authorized examples of the most unfeeling barbarity. Surely, the groans of the weak, sacrificed to the cruel ignorance and indolence of the powerful; the barbarous torments lavished and multiplied with useless severity, for crimes either not proved, or in their nature impossible; the filth and horrors of a prison, increased by the most cruel tormentor of the miserable, uncertainty, ought to have roused the attention of those, whose business is to direct the opinions of mankind.

The immortal *Montesquieu* has but slightly touched on this subject. Truth, which is eternally the same, has obliged me to follow the steps of that great man; but the studious part of mankind, for whom I write, will easily distinguish the superstructure from the foundation. I shall be happy, if, with him, I can obtain the secret thanks of the obscure and peaceful disciples of reason and philosophy, and excite that tender emotion, in which sensible minds sympathise with him who pleads the cause of humanity.

OF THE ORIGIN OF PUNISHMENTS.

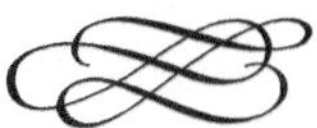

LAWS are the conditions under which men, naturally independent, united themselves in society. Weary of living in a continual state of war, and of enjoying a liberty which became of little value, from the uncertainty of its duration, they sacrificed one part of it to enjoy the rest in peace and security. The sum of all these portions of the liberty of each individual constituted the sovereignty of a nation; and was deposited in the hands of the sovereign, as the lawful administrator. But it was not sufficient only to establish this deposit; it was also necessary to defend it from the usurpation of each individual, who will always endeavour to take away from the mass, not only his own portion, but to encroach on that of others. Some motives, therefore, that strike the senses, were necessary to prevent the despotism of each individual from plunging society into its former chaos. Such motives are the punishment established against the infractors of the laws. I say that motives of this kind are necessary; because experience shews that, the multitude adopt no established rules of conduct; and because, society is prevented from approaching to that dissolution (to which, as well as all other parts of the physical and moral world, it naturally tends) only by motives that are the immediate objects of sense, and which, being continually presented to the mind, are sufficient to counterbalance the effects of the passions of the individual which oppose the general good. Neither the power of eloquence, nor the sublimest truths, are sufficient to restrain, for any length of time, those passions which are excited by the lively impression of present objects.

OF THE RIGHT TO PUNISH.

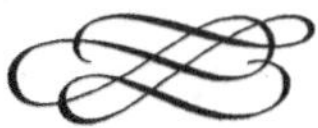

EVERY punishment which does not arise from absolute necessity, says the great *Montesquieu*, is tyrannical. A proposition which may be made more general, thus. Every act of authority of one man over another, for which there is not an absolute necessity, is tyrannical. It is upon this, then, that the sovereign's right to punish crimes is founded; that is, upon the necessity of defending the public liberty, intrusted to his care, from the usurpation of individuals; and punishments are just in proportion as the liberty, preserved by the sovereign, is sacred and valuable.

Let us consult the human heart, and there we shall find the foundation of the sovereign's right to punish; for no advantage in moral policy can be lasting, which is not founded on the indeliable sentiments of the heart of man. Whatever law deviates from this principle will always meet with a resistance, which will destroy it in the end; for the smallest force, continually applied, will overcome the most violent motion communicated to bodies.

No man ever gave up his liberty merely for the good of the public. Such a chimera exists only in romances. Every individual wishes, if possible, to be exempt from the compacts that bind the rest of mankind.

The multiplication of mankind, though slow, being too great for the means which the earth, in its natural state, offered to satisfy necessities, which every day became more numerous, obliged men to separate again, and form new societies. These naturally opposed the first, and a state of war was transferred from individuals to nations.

Thus it was necessity that forced men to give up a part of their liberty; it is certain, then, that every individual would choose to put into the public stock the smallest portion possible; as much only as was sufficient to engage others to defend it. The aggregate of these, the smallest portions possible, forms the right of punishing: all that extends beyond this is abuse, not justice.

Observe, that by *justice* I understand nothing more than that bond, which is necessary to keep the interest of individuals united; without which, men would return to the original state of barbarity. All punishments, which exceed the necessity of preserving this bond, are in their nature unjust. We should be cautious how we associate with the word *justice*, an idea of anything real, such as a physical power, or a being that actually exists. I do not, by any means, speak of the justice of God, which is of another kind, and refers immediately to rewards and punishments in a life to come.

CONSEQUENCES OF THE FOREGOING PRINCIPLES.

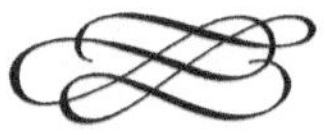

THE laws only can determine the punishment of crimes; and the authority of making penal laws can only reside with the legislator, who represents the whole society united by the social compact. No magistrate then, (as he is one of the society,) can, with justice, inflict on any other member of the same society, punishment that is not ordained by the laws. But as a punishment, increased beyond the degree fixed by the law, is the just punishment, with the addition of another; it follows, that no magistrate, even under a pretence of zeal, or the public good, should increase the punishment already determined by the laws.

If every individual be bound to society, society is equally bound to him by a contract, which, from its nature, equally binds both parties. This obligation, which descends from the throne to the cottage, and equally binds the highest and lowest of mankind, signifies nothing more, than that it is the interest of all, that conventions, which are useful to the greatest number, should be punctually observed. The violation of this compact by any individual, is an introduction to anarchy.

The sovereign, who represents the society itself, can only make general laws to bind the members; but it belongs not to him to judge whether any individual has violated the social compact, or incurred the punishment in consequence. For in this case there are two parties, one represented by the sovereign, who insists upon the violation of the contract, and the other is the person accused, who denies it. It is necessary then that there should be a third person to decide this contest; that is to say, a judge, or magistrate, from whose determination there should be no appeal; and this determination should consist of a simple affirmation, or negation of fact.

If it can only be proved, that the severity of punishments, though not immediately contrary to the public good, or to the end for which they were intended, *viz.*, to prevent crimes, be useless; then such severity would be contrary to those beneficent virtues, which are the consequence of enlightened reason, which instructs the sovereign to wish rather to govern men in a state of freedom and happiness, than of slavery. It would also be contrary to justice, and the social compact.

OF THE INTERPRETATION OF LAWS.

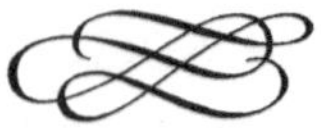

JUDGES, in criminal cases, have no right to interpret the penal laws, because they are not legislators. They have not received the laws from our ancestors as a domestic tradition, or as the will of a testator, which his heirs and executors are to obey; but they receive them from a society actually existing, or from the sovereign, its representative. Even the authority of the laws is not founded on any pretended obligation, or ancient convention; which must be null, as it cannot bind those who did not exist at the time of its institution; and unjust, as it would reduce men, in the ages following, to a herd of brutes, without any power of judging or acting. The laws receive their force and authority from an oath of fidelity, either tacit or expressed, which living subjects have sworn to their sovereign, in order to restrain the intestine fermentation of the private interests of individuals. From hence springs their true and natural authority. Who then is their lawful interpreter? The sovereign, that is, the representative of society, and not the judge, whose office is only to examine, if a man have or have not, committed an action contrary to the laws.

In every criminal cause the judge should reason syllogistically. The *major* should be the general law; the *minor* the conformity of the action, or its opposition to the laws; the *conclusion,* liberty or punishment. If the judge be obliged by the imperfection of the laws, or chooses to make any other, or more syllogisms than this, it will be an introduction to uncertainty.

There is nothing more dangerous than the common axiom: *the spirit of the laws is to be considered.* To adopt it is to give way to the torrent of opinions. This may seem a paradox to vulgar minds, which are more strongly affected by the smallest disorder before their eyes, than by the most pernicious, though remote, consequences produced by one false principle adopted by a nation.

Our knowledge is in proportion to the number of our ideas. The more complex these are, the greater is the variety of positions in which they may be considered. Every man hath his own particular point of view, and at different times sees the same objects in very different lights. The spirit of the laws will then be the result of the good or bad logic of the judge; and this will depend on his good or bad digestion; on the violence of his passions; on the rank and condition of the abused, or on his connections with the judge; and on all those circumstances which change the appearance of objects in the fluctuating mind of man. Hence we see the fate of a delinquent changed many times in passing through the different courts of judicature, and his life and liberty victims to the false ideas or ill humour of the judge; who mistakes the vague result of his own confused reasoning, for the just interpretation of the laws. We see the same crimes punished in a different manner at different times in the same tribunals; the consequence of not having consulted the constant and invariable voice of the laws, but the erring instability of arbitrary interpretation.

The disorders that may arise from a rigorous observance of the letter of penal laws, are not to be compared with those produced by the interpretation of them. The first are temporary inconveniencies, which will oblige the legislator to correct the letter of the law, the want of preciseness and uncertainty of which has occasioned these disorders; and this will put a stop to the fatal liberty of explaining; the source of arbitrary and venal declamations. When the code of laws is once fixed, it should be observed in the literal sense, and nothing more is left to the judge than to determine, whether an action be, or be not, conformable to the written law. When the rule of right, which ought to direct the actions of the philosopher as well as the ignorant, is a matter of controversy, not of fact, the people are slaves to the magistrates. The despotism of this multitude of tyrants is more insupportable, the less the distance is between the oppressor and the oppressed; more fatal than that of one, for the tyranny of many is not to be shaken off, but by having recourse to that of one alone. It is more cruel, as it meets with more opposition, and the cruelty of a tyrant is not in proportion to his strength, but to the obstacles that oppose him.

These are the means by which security of person and property is best obtained; which is just, as it is the purpose of uniting in society; and it is useful, as each person may calculate exactly the inconveniencies attending every crime. By these means subjects will acquire a spirit of independence and liberty; however it may appear to those who dare to call the weakness of submitting blindly to their capricious and interested opinions by the sacred name of virtue.

These principles will displease those who have made it a rule with themselves, to transmit to their inferiors the tyranny they suffer from their superiors. I should have every thing to fear, if tyrants were to read my book; but tyrants never read.

OF THE OBSCURITY OF LAWS.

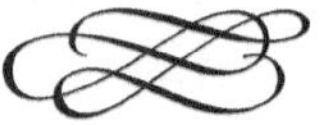

IF the power of interpreting laws be an evil, obscurity in them must be another, as the former is the consequence of the latter. This evil will be still greater, if the laws be written in a language unknown to the people; who, being ignorant of the consequences of their own actions, become necessarily dependent on a few, who are interpreters of the laws, which, instead of being public and general, are thus rendered private and particular. What must we think of mankind when we reflect, that such is the established custom of the greatest part of our polished and enlightened Europe? Crimes will be less frequent, in proportion as the code of laws is more universally read, and understood; for there is no doubt, but that the eloquence of the passions is greatly assisted by the ignorance and uncertainty of punishments.

Hence it follows, that without written laws, no society will ever acquire a fixed form of government, in which the power is vested in the whole, and not in any part of the society; and in which the laws are not to be altered but by the will of the whole, nor corrupted by the force of private interest. Experience and reason shew us, that the probability of human traditions diminishes in proportion as they are distant from their sources. How then can laws resist the inevitable force of time, if there be not a lasting monument of the social compact?

Hence we see the use of printing, which alone makes the public, and not a few individuals, the guardians and defenders of the laws. It is this art which, by diffusing literature, has gradually dissipated the gloomy spirit of cabal and intrigue. To this art it is owing, that the atrocious crimes of our ancestors, who were alternately slaves and tyrants, are become less frequent. Those who are acquainted with the history of the two or three last centuries, may observe, how from the lap of luxury and effeminacy have sprung the most tender virtues, humanity, benevolence, and toleration of human errors. They may contemplate the effects of, what was so improperly called, ancient simplicity and good faith; humanity groaning under implacable superstition; the avarice and ambition of a few, staining with human blood the thrones and palaces of kings; secret treasons and public massacres; every noble a tyrant over the people; and the ministers of the gospel of Christ bathing their hands in blood, in the name of the God of all mercy. We may talk as we please of the corruption and degeneracy of the present age, but happily we see no such horrid examples of cruelty and oppression.

OF THE PROPORTION
BETWEEN CRIMES AND
PUNISHMENTS.

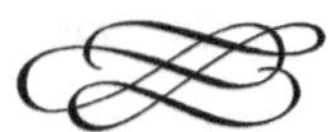

IT is not only the common interest of mankind that crimes should not be committed, but that crimes of every kind should be less frequent, in proportion to the evil they produce to society Therefore, the means made use of by the legislature to prevent crimes, should be more powerful, in proportion as they are destructive of the public safety and happiness, and as the inducements to commit them are stronger. Therefore there ought to be a fixed proportion between crimes and punishments.

It is impossible to prevent entirely all the disorders which the passions of mankind cause in society. These disorders increase in proportion to the number of people, and the opposition of private interests. If we consult history, we shall find them increasing, in every state, with the extent of dominion. In political arithmetic, it is necessary to substitute a calculation of probabilities to mathematical exactness. That force which continually impels us to our own private interest, like gravity, acts incessantly, unless it meets with an obstacle to oppose it. The effects of this force are the confused series of human actions. Punishments, which I would call political obstacles, prevent the fatal effects of private interest, without destroying the impelling cause, which is that sensibility inseparable from man. The legislator acts, in this case, like a skilful architect, who endeavours to counteract the force of gravity by combining the circumstances which may contribute to the strength of his edifice.

The necessity of uniting in society being granted, together with the conventions, which the opposite interests of individuals must necessarily require, a scale of crimes may be formed, of which the first degree should consist of those which immediately tend to the dissolution of society, and the last, of the smallest possible injustice done to a private member of that society. Between these extremes will be comprehended, all actions contrary to the public good, which are called criminal, and which descend by insensible degrees, decreasing from the highest to the lowest. If mathematical calculation could be applied to the obscure and infinite combinations of human actions, there might be a corresponding scale of punishments, descending from the greatest to the least; but it will be sufficient that the wise legislator mark the principal divisions, without disturbing the order, lest to crimes of the *first* degree, be assigned punishments of the *last*. If there were an exact and universal scale of crimes and punishments, we should then have a common measure of the degree of liberty and slavery, humanity and cruelty, of different nations.

Any action, which is not comprehended in the above mentioned scale, will not be called a crime, or punished as such, except by those who have an interest in the denomination. The uncertainty of the extreme points of this scale, hath produced a system of morality which contradicts the laws; a multitude of laws that contradict each other; and many which expose the best men to the severest punishments, rendering the ideas of *vice* and *virtue* vague and fluctuating, and even their existence doubtful. Hence that fatal lethargy of political bodies, which terminates in their destruction.

Whoever reads, with a philosophic eye, the history of nations, and their laws, will generally find, that the ideas of virtue and vice, of a good or a bad citizen, change with the revolution of ages; not in proportion to the alteration of circumstances, and consequently conformable to the common good; but in proportion to the passions and errors by which the different lawgivers were successively influenced. He will frequently observe, that the passions and vices of one age, are the foundation of the morality of the following; that violent passion, the offspring of fanaticism and enthusiasm, being weakened by time, which reduces all the phenomena of the natural and moral world to an equality, become, by degrees, the prudence of the age, and an useful instrument in the hands of the powerful or artful politician. Hence the uncertainty of our notions of honour and virtue; an uncertainty which will ever remain, because they change with the revolutions of time, and names survive the things they originally signified; they change with the boundaries of states, which are often the same both in physical and moral geography.

Pleasure and pain are the only springs of action in beings endowed with sensibility. Even among the motives which incite men to acts of religion, the invisible Legislator has ordained rewards and punishments. From a partial distribution of these will arise that contradiction, so little observed, because so common; I mean, that of punishing by the laws the crimes which the laws have occasioned. If an equal punishment be ordained for two crimes that injure society in different degrees, there is nothing to deter men from committing the greater, as often as it is attended with greater advantage.

OF ESTIMATING THE DEGREE
OF CRIMES.

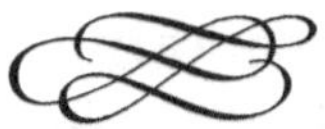

THE foregoing reflections authorise me to assert, that crimes are only to be measured by the injury done to society.

They err, therefore, who imagine that a crime is greater, or less, according to the intention of the person by whom it is committed; for this will depend on the actual impression of objects on the senses, and on the previous disposition of the mind; both which will vary in different persons, and even in the same person at different times, according to the succession of ideas, passions, and circumstances. Upon that system, it would be necessary to form, not only a particular code for every individual, but a new penal law for every crime. Men, often with the best intention, do the greatest injury to society, and with the worst, do it the most essential services.

Others have estimated crimes rather by the dignity of the person offended, than by their consequences to society. If this were the true standard, the smallest irreverence to the divine Being ought to be punished with infinitely more severity, than the assassination of a monarch.

In short, others have imagined, that the greatness of the sin should aggravate the crime. But the fallacy of this opinion will appear on the slightest consideration of the relations between man and man, and between God and man. The relations between man and man are relations of equality. Necessity alone hath produced, from the opposition of private passions and interests, the idea of public utility, which is the foundation of human justice. The other are relations of dependence, between an imperfect creature and his Creator, the most perfect of beings, who has reserved to himself the sole right of being both lawgiver and judge; for he alone can, without injustice, be, at the same time, both one and the other. If he hath decreed eternal punishments for those who disobey his will, shall an insect dare to put himself in the place of divine justice, to pretend to punish for the Almighty, who is himself all-sufficient; who cannot receive impressions of pleasure or pain, and who alone, of all other beings, acts without being acted upon? The degree of sin depends on the malignity of the heart, which is impenetrable to finite being. How then can the degree of sin serve as a standard to determine the degree of crimes? If that were admitted, men may punish when God pardons, and pardon when God condemns; and thus act in opposition to the Supreme Being.

OF THE DIVISION OF CRIMES.

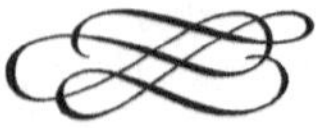

WE have proved, then, that crimes are to be estimated by *the injury done to society.* This is one of those palpable truths, which, though evident to the meanest capacity, yet, by a combination of circumstances, are only known to a few thinking men in every nation, and in every age. But opinions, worthy only of the despotism of Asia, and passions armed with power and authority, have, generally by insensible and sometimes by violent impressions on the timid credulity of men, effaced those simple ideas which perhaps constituted the first philosophy of infant society. Happily the philosophy of the present enlightened age seems again to conduct us to the same principles, and with that degree of certainty which is obtained by a rational examination, and repeated experience.

A scrupulous adherence to order would require, that we should now examine and distinguish the different species of crimes, and the modes of punishment; but they are so variable in their nature, from the different circumstances of ages and countries, that the detail would be tiresome and endless. It will be sufficient for my purpose, to point out the most general principles, and the most common and dangerous errors, in order to undeceive, as well those who, from a mistaken zeal for liberty, would introduce anarchy and confusion, as those who pretend to reduce society in general to the regularity of a convent.

Some crimes are immediately destructive of society, or its representative; others attack the private security of the life, property or honour of individuals; and a third class consists of such actions as are contrary to the laws which relate to the general good of the community.

The first, which are of the highest degree, as they are most destructive to society, are called crimes of *Leze-majesty*.[1] Tyranny and ignorance, which have confounded the clearest terms and ideas, have given this appellation to crimes of a different nature, and consequently have established the same punishment for each; and on this occasion, as on a thousand others, men have been sacrificed victims to a word. Every crime, even of the most private nature, injures society; but every crime does not threaten its immediate destruction. Moral, as well as physical actions, have their sphere of activity differently circumscribed, like all the movements of nature, by time and space; it is therefore a sophistical interpretation, the common philosophy of slaves, that would confound the limits of things established by eternal truth.

To these succeed crimes which are destructive of the security of individuals. This security being the principal end of all society, and to which every citizen hath an undoubted right, it becomes indispensably necessary, that to these crimes the greatest of punishments should be assigned.

The opinion, that every member of society has a right to do anything that is not contrary to the laws, without fearing any other inconveniencies than those which are the natural consequences of the action itself, is a political dogma, which should be defended by the laws, inculcated by the magistrates, and believed by the people; a sacred dogma, without which there can be no lawful society; a just recompence for our sacrifice of that universal liberty of action, common to all sensible beings, and only limited by our natural powers. By this principle, our minds become free, active and vigorous; by this alone we are inspired with that virtue which knows no fear, so different from that pliant prudence worthy of those only who can bear a precarious existence.

Attempts, therefore, against the life and liberty of a citizen, are crimes of the highest nature. Under this head we comprehend not only assassinations and robberies committed by the populace, but by grandees and magistrates; whose example acts with more force, and at a greater distance, destroying the ideas of justice and duty among the subjects, and substituting that of the right of the strongest, equally dangerous to those who exercise it, and to those who suffer.

----

1. High-treason.

OF HONOUR.

THERE is a remarkable difference between the civil laws, those jealous guardians of life and property, and the laws of, what is called, *honour,* which particularly respects the opinion of others.

Honour is a term which has been the foundation of many long and brilliant reasonings, without annexing to it any precise or fixed idea. How miserable is the condition of the human mind, to which the most distant and least essential matters, the revolution of the heavenly bodies, are more distinctly known, than the most interesting truths of morality, which are always confused and fluctuating, as they happen to be driven by the gales of passion, or received and transmitted by ignorance! But this will cease to appear strange, if it be considered, that as objects, when too near the eye, appear confused, so the too great vicinity of the ideas of morality, is the reason why the simple ideas, of which they are composed, are easily confounded; but which must be separated, before we can investigate the phenomena of human sensibility; and the intelligent observer of human nature will cease to be surprised, that so many ties, and such an apparatus of morality are necessary to the security and happiness of mankind.

Honour, then, is one of those complex ideas, which are an aggregate not only of simple ones, but of others so complicated, that, in their various modes of affecting the human mind, they sometimes exclude part of the elements of which they are composed; retaining only some few of the most common, as many algebraic quantities admit one common divisor. To find this common divisor of the different ideas attached to the word honour, it will be necessary to go back to the original formation of society.

The first laws, and the first magistrates, owed their existence to the necessity of preventing the disorders, which the natural despotism of individuals would unavoidably produce. This was the object of the establishment of society, and was either in reality or in appearance, the principal design of all codes of laws, even the most pernicious. But the more intimate connections of men, and the progress of their knowledge, gave rise to an infinite number of necessities, and mutual acts of friendship, between the members of society. These necessities were not foreseen by the laws, and could not be satisfied by the actual power of each individual. At this epocha began to be established the despotism of opinion, as being the only means of obtaining those benefits which the law could not procure, and of removing those evils against which the laws were no security. It is opinion, that tormentor of the wise and the ignorant, that has exalted the appearance of virtue above virtue itself. Hence the esteem of men becomes not only useful, but necessary, to every one, to prevent his sinking below the common level. The ambitious man grasps at it, as being necessary to his designs; the vain man sues for it, as a testimony of his merit; the honest man demands it as his due; and the most men consider it as necessary to their existence.

Honour, being produced after the formation of society, could not be a part of the common deposite, and therefore, whilst we act under its influence, we return, for that instant, to a state of nature, and withdraw ourselves from the laws, which in this case are insufficient for our protection.

Hence it follows, that in extreme political liberty, and in absolute despotism, all ideas of honour disappear, or are confounded with others. In the first case, reputation becomes useless from the despotism of the laws; and in the second the despotism of one man, annulling civil existence, reduces the rest to a precarious and temporary personality. Honour, then, is one of the fundamental principles of those monarchies, which are a limited despotism, and in these, like revolutions in despotic states, it is a momentary return to a state of nature, and original equality.

OF DUELLING.

FROM the necessity of the esteem of others, have arisen single combats, and they have been established by the anarchy of the laws. They are thought to have been unknown to the ancients; perhaps because they did not assemble in their temples, in their theatres, or with their friends, suspiciously armed with swords; and, perhaps, because single combats were a common spectacle, exhibited to the people by gladiators, who were slaves, and whom freemen disdained to imitate.

In vain have the laws endeavoured to abolish this custom, by punishing the offenders with death. A man of honour, deprived of the esteem of others, foresees that he must be reduced, either to a solitary existence, insupportable to a social creature, or become the object of perpetual insult; considerations sufficient to overcome the fear of death.

What is the reason that duels are not so frequent among the common people, as amongst the great?

Not only because they do not wear swords, but because to men of that class reputation is of less importance than it is to those of a higher rank, who commonly regard each other with distrust and jealousy.

It may not be without its use to repeat here, what has been mentioned by other writers, *viz.*, that the best method of preventing this crime is to punish the aggressor, that is, the person who gave occasion to the duel, and to acquit him, who, without any fault on his side, is obliged to defend that, which is not sufficiently secured to him by the laws.

OF CRIMES WHICH DISTURB THE PUBLIC TRANQUILLITY.

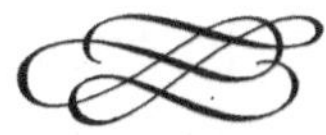

ANOTHER class of crimes are those which disturb the public tranquillity and the quiet of the citizens; such as tumults and riots in the public streets, which are intended for commerce and the passage of the inhabitants; the discourses of fanatics, which rouse the passions of the curious multitude, and gain strength from the number of their hearers, who, though deaf to calm and solid reasoning, are always affected by obscure and mysterious enthusiasm.

The illumination of the streets, during the night, at the public expense; guards stationed in different quarters of the city; the plain and moral discourses of religion, reserved for the silence and tranquillity of churches, and protected by authority; and harangues in support of the interest of the public, delivered only at the general meetings of the nation, in parliament, or where the sovereign resides; are all means to prevent the dangerous effects of the misguided passions of the people These should be the principal objects of the vigilance of a magistrate, and which the French call *Police;* but if this magistrate should act in an arbitrary manner, and not in conformity to the code of laws, which ought to be in the hand of every member of the community, he opens a door to tyranny, which always surrounds the confines of political liberty.

I do not know of any exception to this general axiom, that *Every member of the society should know when he is criminal, and when innocent.* If censors, and, in general, arbitrary magistrates, be necessary in any government, it proceeds from some fault in the constitution. The uncertainty of crimes hath sacrificed more victims to secret tyranny, than have ever suffered by public and solemn cruelty.

What are, in general, the proper punishments for crimes? Is the punishment of death, really *useful,* or necessary for the safety or good order of society? Are tortures and torments consistent with *justice,* or do they answer the *end* proposed by the laws? Which is the best method of preventing crimes? Are the same punishments equally useful at all times? What influence have they on manners? These problems should be solved with that geometrical precision which the mist of sophistry, the seduction of eloquence, and the timidity of doubt are unable to resist.

If I have no other merit than that of having first presented to my country, with a greater degree of evidence, what other nations have written, and are beginning to practise, I shall account myself fortunate; but if, by supporting the rights of mankind

and of invincible truth, I shall contribute to save
from the agonies of death one unfortunate victim of
tyranny, or of ignorance, equally fatal; his blessings,
and tears of transport, will be a sufficient consolation to me for the contempt of all mankind.

OF THE INTENT OF PUNISHMENTS.

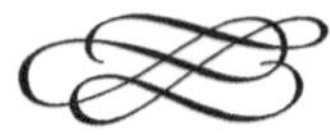

FROM the foregoing considerations it is evident, that the intent of punishments is not to torment a sensible being, nor to undo a crime already committed. Is it possible that torments, and useless cruelty, the instruments of furious fanaticism, or of impotency of tyrants, can be authorized by a political body? which, so far from being influenced by passion, should be the cool moderator of the passions of individuals. Can the groans of a tortured wretch recal the time past, or reverse the crime he has committed?

The end of punishment, therefore, is no other, than to prevent others from committing the like offence. Such punishments, therefore, and such a mode of inflicting them, ought to be chosen, as will make strongest and most lasting impressions on the minds of others, with the least torment to the body of the criminal.

OF THE CREDIBILITY OF WITNESSES.

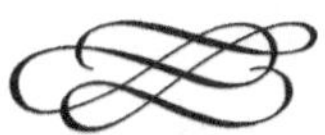

TO determine exactly the credibility of a witness, and the force of evidence, is an important point in every good legislation. Every man of common sense, that is, every one whose ideas have some connexion with each other, and whose sensations are conformable to those of other men, may be a witness; but the credibility of his evidence will be in proportion as he is interested in declaring or concealing the truth. Hence it appears, how frivolous is the reasoning of those, who reject the testimony of women on account of their weakness; how puerile it is, not to admit the evidence of those who are under sentence of death, because they are dead in law; and how irrational, to exclude persons branded with infamy: for in all these cases they ought to be credited, when they have no interest in giving false testimony.

The credibility of a witness, then, should only diminish in proportion to the hatred, friendship, or connexions subsisting between him and the delinquent. One witness is not sufficient; for whilst the accused denies what the other affirms, truth remains suspended, and the right that every one has to be believed innocent, turns the balance in his favour.

The credibility of a witness is the less, as the atrociousness of the crime is greater, from the improbability of its having been committed; as in cases of witchcraft, and acts of wanton cruelty. The writers on penal laws have adopted a contrary principle, *viz.*, that the credibility of a witness is greater, as the crime is more atrocious. Behold their inhuman maxim, dictated by the most cruel imbecility. *In atrocissimis, leviores conjecturæ sufficiunt, licet judici jura transgredi.* Let us translate this sentence, that mankind may see one of the many unreasonable principles to which they are ignorantly subject. *In the most atrocious crimes the slightest conjectures are sufficient, and the judge is allowed to exceed the limits of the law.* The absurd practices of legislators are often the effect of timidity, which is a principal source of the contradictions of mankind. The legislators, (or rather lawyers, whose opinions, when alive, were interested and venal, but which after their death become of decisive authority, and are sovereign arbiters of the lives and fortunes of men), terrified by the condemnation of some innocent person, have burdened the law with pompous and useless formalities, the scrupulous observance of which will place anarchical impunity on the throne of justice; at other times, perplexed by atrocious crimes of difficult proof, they imagined themselves under a necessity of superseding the very formalities established by themselves; and thus, at one time, with despotic impatience, and at another with feminine timidity, they transform their solemn judgments into a game of hazard.

But to return. In the case of witchcraft, it is much more probable, that a number of men should be deceived, than that any person should exercise a power which God hath refused to every created being. In like manner, in cases of wanton cruelty, the presumption is always against the accuser, without some motive of fear or hate. There are no spontaneous or superfluous sentiments in the heart of man; they are all the result of impressions on the senses.

The credibility of a witness may also be diminished, by his being a member of a private society, whose customs and principles of conduct are either not known, or are different from those of the public. Such a man has not only his own passions, but those of the society of which he is a member.

Finally, the credibility of a witness is null, when the question relates to the words of a criminal; for the tone of voice, the gesture, all that precedes, accompanies and follows the different ideas which men annex to the same words, may so alter and modify a man's discourse, that it is almost impossible to repeat them precisely in the manner in which they were spoken. Besides, violent and uncommon actions, such as real crimes, leave a trace in the multitude of circumstances that attend them, and in their effects; but words remain only in the memory of the hearers, who are commonly negli-

gent or prejudiced. It is infinitely easier then to
found an accusation on the words, than on the actions of a man; for in these, the number of circumstances, urged against the accused, afford him
variety of means of justification.

OF EVIDENCE AND THE PROOFS OF A CRIME, AND OF THE FORM OF JUDGMENT.

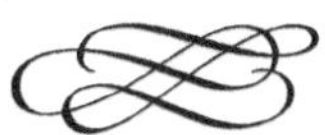

THE following general theorem is of great use in determining the certainty of fact. When the proofs of a crime are dependent on each other, that is, when the evidence of each witness, taken separately, proves nothing; or when all the proofs are dependent upon one, the number of proofs neither increase nor diminish the probability of the fact; for the force of the whole is no greater than the force of that on which they depend; and if this fails, they all fall to the ground. When the proofs are independent on each other, the probability of the fact increases in proportion to the number of proofs; for the falsehood of one does not diminish the veracity of another.

It may seem extraordinary that I speak of probability with regard to crimes, which, to deserve a punishment, must be certain. But this paradox will vanish, when it is considered, that, strictly speaking, moral certainty is only probability; but which is called a certainty, because every man in his senses assents to it from an habit produced by the necessity of acting, and which is anterior to all speculation. That certainty which is necessary to decide that the accused is guilty, is the very same which determines every man in the most important transactions of his life.

The proofs of a crime may be divided into two classes, perfect and imperfect. I call those perfect which exclude the possibility of innocence; imperfect, those which do not exclude this possibility. Of the first, one only is sufficient for condemnation; of the second, as many are required as form a perfect proof: that is to say, that though each of these, separately taken, does not exclude the possibility of innocence, it is nevertheless excluded by their union. It should be also observed, that the imperfect proofs of which the accused, if innocent, might clear himself, and does not, become perfect.

But it is much easier to feel this moral certainty of proofs, than to define it exactly. For this reason, I think it an excellent law which establishes assistants to the principal judge, and those chosen by lot; for that ignorance, which judges by its feelings, is less subject to error, than the knowledge of the laws which judges by opinion. Where the laws are clear and precise, the office of the judge is merely to ascertain the fact. If, in examining the proofs of a crime, acuteness and dexterity be required; if clearness and precision be necessary in summing up the result; to judge of the result itself, nothing is wanting but plain and ordinary good sense, a less fallacious guide than the knowledge of a judge accustomed to find guilty, and to reduce all things to an artificial system, borrowed from his studies. Happy the nation, where the knowledge of the law is not a science!

It is an admirable law which ordains, that every man shall be tried by his peers; for when life, liberty and fortune are in question, the sentiments, which a difference of rank and fortune inspire, should be silent; that superiority with which the fortunate look upon the unfortunate, and that envy with which the inferior regard their superiors, should have no influence. But when the crime is an offence against a fellow-subject, one half of the judges should be peers to the accused, and the other peers to the person offended. So that all private interest, which, in spite of ourselves, modifies the appearance of objects, even in the eyes of the most equitable, is counteracted, and nothing remains to turn aside the direction of truth and the laws. It is also just, that the accused should have the liberty of excluding a certain number of his judges. Where this liberty is enjoyed for a long time, without any instance to the contrary, the criminal seems to condemn himself.

All trials should be public, that opinion, which is the best, or, perhaps, the only cement of society, may curb the authority of the powerful, and the passions of the judge; and that the people may say, "We are protected by the laws; we are not slaves;" a sentiment which inspires courage, and which is the

best tribute to a sovereign who knows his real interest. I shall not enter into particulars. There may be
some persons who expect that I should say all that
can be said upon this subject; to such, what I have
already written must be unintelligible.

OF SECRET ACCUSATIONS.

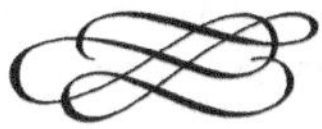

SECRET accusations are a manifest abuse, but consecrated by custom in many nations, where, from the weakness of the government, they are necessary. This custom makes men false and treacherous. Whoever suspects another to be an informer, beholds in him an enemy; and, from thence, mankind are accustomed to disguise their real sentiments; and from the habit of concealing them from others, they at last even hide them from themselves. Unhappy are those, who have arrived at this point! Without any certain and fixed principles to guide them, they fluctuate in the vast sea of opinion, and are busied only in escaping the monsters which surround them; to those, the present is always embittered by the uncertainty of the future; deprived of the pleasures of tranquillity and security, some fleeting moments of happiness, scattered thinly through their wretched lives, console them for the misery of existing. Shall we, amongst such men, find intrepid soldiers to defend their king and country? Amongst such men shall we find incorruptible magistrates, who, with the spirit of freedom and patriotic eloquence, will support and explain the true interest of their sovereign; who, with the tributes, offer up at the throne the love and blessing of the people, and thus bestow on the palaces of the great, and the humble cottage, peace and security; and to the industrious a prospect of bettering their lot, that useful ferment and vital principle of states?

Who can defend himself from calumny, armed with that impenetrable shield of tyranny, secrecy? What a miserable government must that be, where the sovereign suspects an enemy in every subject, and, to secure the tranquillity of the public, is obliged to sacrifice the repose of every individual?

By what arguments is it pretended, that *secret accusations* may be justified? The public safety, say they, and the security and maintenance of the established form of government. But what a strange constitution is that, where the government, which hath in its favour not only power but opinion, still more efficacious, yet fears its own subjects? *The indemnity of the informer.* Do not the laws defend him sufficiently; and are there subjects more powerful than the laws? *The necessity of protecting the informer from infamy.* When secret calumny is authorised, and punished only when public. *The nature of the crime.* If actions, indifferent in themselves, or even useful to the public, were called crimes, both the accusation and the trial could never be too secret. But can there be any crime, committed against the public, which ought not to be publicly punished? I respect all governments; and I speak not of any one in particular. Such may sometimes be the nature of circumstances, that when abuses are inherent in the constitution, it may be imagined, that to rectify them, would be to destroy the constitution itself. But were I to dictate new laws in a remote corner of the universe, the good of posterity, ever present to my mind, would hold back my trembling hand, and prevent me from authorising *secret accusations.*

Public accusations, says *Montesquieu,* are more conformable to the nature of a republic, where zeal for the public good is the principal passion of a citizen, than of a monarchy, in which, as this sentiment is very feeble, from the nature of the government, the best establishment is that of *commissioners,* who, in the name of the public, accuse the infractors of the laws. But in all governments as well in a republic as in a monarchy, the punishment, due to the crime of which one accuses another, ought to be inflicted on the informer.

OF TORTURE.

THE torture of a criminal, during the course of his trial, is a cruelty, consecrated by custom in most nations. It is used with an intent either to make him confess his crime, or explain some contradictions, into which he had been led during his examination; or discover his accomplices; or for some kind of metaphysical and incomprehensible purgation of infamy; or, finally, in order to discover other crimes, of which he is not accused, but of which he may be guilty.

No man can be judged a criminal until he be found guilty; nor can society take from him the public protection, until it have been proved that he has violated the conditions on which it was granted. What right, then, but that of power, can authorise the punishment of a citizen, so long as there remains any doubt of his guilt? The dilemma is frequent. Either he is guilty, or not guilty. If guilty, he should only suffer the punishment ordained by the laws, and torture becomes useless, as his confession is unnecessary. If he be not guilty, you torture the innocent; for, in the eye of the law, every man is innocent, whose crime has not been proved. Besides, it is confounding all relations, to expect that a man should be both the accuser and accused; and that pain should be the test of truth, as if truth resided in the muscles and fibres of a wretch in torture. By this method, the robust will escape, and the feeble be condemned. These are the inconveniencies of this pretended test of truth, worthy only of a cannibal; and which the Romans, in many respects barbarous, and whose savage virtue has been too much admired, reserved for the slaves alone.

What is the political intention of punishments? To terrify, and to be an example to others. Is this intention answered, by thus privately torturing the guilty and the innocent? It is doubtless of importance, that no crime should remain unpunished; but it is useless to make a public example of the author of a crime hid in darkness. A crime already committed, and for which there can be no remedy, can only be punished by a political society, with an intention that no hopes of impunity should induce others to commit the same. If it be true, that the number of those, who, from fear or virtue, respect the laws, is greater than of those by whom they are violated, the risk of torturing an innocent person is greater, as there is a greater probability that, *cæteris paribus,* an individual hath observed, than that he hath infringed the laws.

There is another ridiculous motive for torture, namely, *to purge a man from infamy.* Ought such an abuse to be tolerated in the eighteenth century? Can pain, which is a sensation, have any connection with a moral sentiment, a matter of opinion? Perhaps the rack may be considered as a refiner's furnace.

It is not difficult to trace this senseless law to its origin; for an absurdity, adopted by a whole nation, must have some affinity with other ideas, established and respected by the same nation. This custom seems to be the offspring of religion, by which mankind, in all nations and in all ages, are so generally influenced. We are taught by our infallible church, that those stains of sin, contracted through human frailty, and which have not deserved the eternal anger of the Almighty, are to be purged away, in another life, by an incomprehensible fire. Now infamy is a stain, and if the punishments and fire of purgatory can take away all spiritual stains, why should not the pain of torture take away those of a civil nature? I imagine that the confession of a criminal, which in some tribunals is required, as being essential to his condemnation, has a similar origin, and has been taken from the mysterious tribunal of penitence, where the confession of sins is a necessary part of the sacrament. Thus have men abused the unerring light of revelation; and in the times of tractable ignorance, having no other, they naturally had recourse to it on every occasion, making the most remote and absurd applications. Moreover, infamy is a sentiment regulated neither by the laws nor by reason, but entirely by opinion. But torture renders the victim infamous, and therefore cannot take infamy away.

Another intention of torture is, to oblige the supposed criminal to reconcile the contradictions into which he may have fallen during his examination; as if the dread of punishment, the uncertainty of his fate, the solemnity of the court, the majesty of the judge, and the ignorance of the accused, were not abundantly sufficient to account for contradictions, which are so common to men even in a state of tranquillity; and which must necessarily be multiplied by the perturbation of the mind of a man, entirely engaged in the thought of saving himself from imminent danger.

This infamous test of truth is a remaining monument of that ancient and savage legislation, in which trials by fire, by boiling water, or the uncertainty of combats, were called *judgments of God;* as if the links of that eternal chain, whose beginning is in the breast of the first cause of all things, could never be disunited by the institutions of men. The only difference between torture, and trials by fire and boiling water, is, that the event of the first depends on the will of the accused; and of the second, on a fact entirely physical and external: but this difference is apparent only, not real. A man on the rack, in the convulsions of torture, has it as little in his power to declare the truth, as, in former times, to prevent, without fraud, the effect of fire or of boiling water.

Every act of the will is invariably in proportion to the force of the impression on our senses. The impression of pain, then, may increase to such a degree, that, occupying the mind entirely, it will compel the sufferer to use the shortest method of freeing himself from torment. His answer, therefore, will be an effect as necessary as that of fire or boiling water; and he will accuse himself of crimes of which he is innocent. So that the very means employed to distinguish the innocent from the guilty, will most effectually destroy all difference between them.

It would be superfluous to confirm these reflections by examples of innocent persons, who from the agony of torture have confessed themselves guilty: innumerable instances may be found in all nations, and in every age. How amazing, that mankind have always neglected to draw the natural conclusion! Lives there a man who, if he have carried his thoughts ever so little beyond the necessities of life, when he reflects on such cruelty, is not tempted to fly from society, and return to his natural state of independence?

The result of torture, then, is a matter of calcution, and depends on the constitution, which differs in every individual, and is in proportion to his strength and sensibility; so that to discover truth by this method, is a problem which may be better resolved by a mathematician than a judge, and may be thus stated: *The force of the muscles, and the sensibility of the nerves of an innocent person being given, it is required to find the degree of pain necessary to make him confess himself guilty of a given crime.*

The examination of the accused is intended to find out the truth; but if this be discovered with so much difficulty, in the air, gesture, and countenance of a man at ease, how can it appear in a countenance distorted by the convulsions of torture. Every violent action destroys those small alterations in the features, which sometimes disclose the sentiments of the heart.

These truths were known to the Roman legislators, amongst whom, as I have already observed, slaves, only, who were not considered as citizens, were tortured. They are known to the English, a nation in which the progress of science, superiority in commerce, riches and power, its natural consequences, together with the numerous examples of virtue and courage, leave no doubt of the excellence of its laws. They have been acknowledged in Sweden, where torture has been abolished. They are known to one of the wisest monarchs in Europe, who, having seated philosophy on the throne, by his beneficent legislation, has made his subjects free, though dependent on the laws; the only freedom that reasonable men can desire in the present state of things. In short, torture has not been thought necessary in the laws of armies, composed chiefly of the dregs of mankind, where its use should seem most necessary. Strange phenomenon! that a set of men, hardened by slaughter, and familiar with blood, should teach humanity to the sons of peace.

It appears also, that these truths were known, though imperfectly, even to those by whom torture has been most frequently practised; for a confession made during torture is null, if it be not afterwards confirmed by an oath; which, if the criminal refuses, he is tortured again. Some civilians, and some nations, permit this infamous *petitio principii* to be only three times repeated, and others leave it to the discretion of the judge; and therefore of two men equally innocent or equally guilty, the most robust and resolute will be acquitted, and the weakest and most pusillanimous will be condemned, in consequence of the following excellent method of reasoning. *I, the judge, must find some one guilty. Thou, who art a strong fellow, hast been able to resist the force of torment; therefore I acquit thee. Thou, being weaker, hath yielded to it; I therefore condemn thee. I am sensible, that the confession which was extorted from thee, has no weight: but if thou dost not confirm by oath what thou hast already confessed, I will have thee tormented again.*

A very strange but necessary consequence of the use of torture, is that the case of the innocent is worse than that of the guilty. With regard to the first, either he confesses the crime, which he has not committed, and is condemned; or he is acquitted, and has suffered a punishment he did not deserve. On the contrary, the person who is really guilty has the most favourable side of the question; for if he supports the torture with firmness and resolution, he is acquitted, and has gained, having exchanged a greater punishment for a less.

The law by which torture is authorised, says, Men, be insensible to pain. Nature has indeed given you an irresistible self-love, and an unalienable right of self-preservation, but I create in you a contrary sentiment, an heroical hatred of yourselves. I command you to accuse yourselves, and to declare the truth, midst the tearing of your flesh and the dislocation of your bones.

Torture is used to discover, whether the criminal be guilty of other crimes besides those of which he is accused: which is equivalent to the following reasoning: Thou art guilty of one crime, therefore it is possible that thou mayst have committed a thousand others: but the affair being doubtful, I must try it by my criterion of truth. The laws order thee to be tormented, because thou art guilty, because thou mayst be guilty, and because I chuse thou shouldst be guilty.

Torture is used to make the criminal discover his accomplices; but if it has been demonstrated that it is not a proper means of discovering truth, how can it serve to discover the accomplices, which is one of the truths required. Will not the man who accuses himself, yet more readily accuse others? Besides, is it just to torment one man for the crime of another? May not the accomplices be found out by the examination of the witnesses, or of the criminal; from the evidence, or from the nature of the crime itself; in short, by all the means that have been used to prove the guilt of the prisoner? The accomplices commonly fly when their comrade is taken. The uncertainty of their fate condemns them to perpetual exile, and frees society from the danger of further injury; whilst the punishment of the criminal, by deterring others, answers the purpose for which it was ordained.

OF PECUNIARY PUNISHMENTS.

THERE was a time when all punishments were pecuniary. The crimes of the subjects were the inheritance of the prince. An injury done to society was a favour to the crown; and the sovereign and magistrates, those guardians of the public security, were interested in the violation of the laws. Crimes were tried, at that time, in a court of Exchequer, and the cause became a civil suit between the person accused and the crown. The magistrate then had other powers than were necessary for the public welfare, and the criminal suffered other punishments than the necessity of example required. The judge was rather a collector for the crown, an agent for the treasury, than a protector and minister of the laws. But, according to this system, for a man to confess himself guilty, was to acknowledge himself a debtor to the crown; which was, and is at present (the effects continuing after the causes have ceased) the intent of all criminal causes. Thus, the criminal who refuses to confess his crime, though convicted by the most undoubted proofs, will suffer a less punishment than if he had confessed; and he will not be put to the torture to oblige him to confess other crimes which he might have committed, as he has not confessed the principal. But the confession being once obtained, the judge becomes master of his body, and torments him with a studied formality, in order to squeeze out of him all the profit possible. Confession, then, is allowed to be a convincing proof, especially when obtained by the force of torture; at the same time that an extra-judicial confession, when a man is at case and under no apprehension, is not sufficient for his condemnation.

All inquiries, which may serve to clear up the fact, but which may weaken the pretensions of the crown, are excluded. It was not from compassion to the criminal, or from considerations of humanity, that torments were sometimes spared, but out of fear of losing those rights which at present appear chimerical and inconceivable. The judge becomes an enemy to the accused, to a wretch, a prey to the horrors of a dungeon, to torture, to death, and an uncertain futurity, more terrible than all; he inquires not into the truth of the fact, but the nature of the crime; he lays snares to make him convict himself; he fears, lest he should not succeed in finding him guilty, and lest that infallibility which every man arrogates to himself should be called in question. It is in the power of the magistrate to determine, what evidence is sufficient to send a man to prison; that he may be proved innocent, he must first be sup-

posed guilty. This is what is called an *offensive* prosecution; and such are all criminal proceedings, in
the eighteenth century, in all parts of our polished
Europe. The true prosecution *for information:* that is,
an impartial inquiry into the fact, that which reason
prescribes, which military laws adopt, and which
Asiatic despotism allows in suits of one subject
against another, is very little practiced in any courts
of justice. What a labyrinth of absurdities! Absurdities which will appear incredible to happier posterity. The philosopher only will be able to read, in the
nature of man, the possibility of there ever having
been such a system.

OF OATHS.

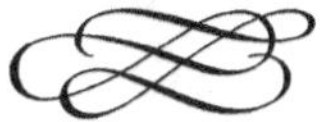

THERE is a palpable contradiction between the laws and the natural sentiments of mankind, in the case of *oaths* which are administered to a criminal to make him speak the truth, when the contrary is his greatest interest. As if a man could think himself obliged to contribute to his own destruction; and as if, when interest speaks, religion was not generally silent; religion, which in all ages hath, of all other things, been most commonly abused; and indeed, upon what motive should it be respected by the wicked, when it has been thus violated by those who were esteemed the wisest of men? The motives which religion opposes to the fear of impending evil, and the love of life, are too weak, as they are too distant, to make any impression on the senses. The affairs of the other world are regulated by laws entirely different from those by which human affairs are directed; why then should we endeavour to compromise matters between them? Why should a man be reduced to the terrible alternative, either of offending God, or of contributing to his own immediate destruction? The laws which require an oath in such a case, leave him only the choice of becoming a bad christian or a martyr. For this reason, oaths become by degrees a mere formality, and all sentiments of religion, perhaps the only motive of honesty in the greatest part of mankind, are destroyed. Experience proves their utility: I appeal to every judge, whether he has ever known that an oath alone has brought truth from the lips of a criminal; and reason tells us, it must be so; for all laws are useless, and, in consequence, destructive, which contradict the natural feelings of mankind. Such laws are like a dyke, opposed directly to the course of a torrent; it is either immediately overwhelmed, or by a whirlpool formed by itself, it is gradually undermined and destroyed.

OF THE ADVANTAGE OF IMMEDIATE PUNISHMENT.

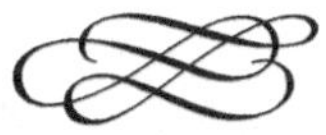

THE more immediately, after the commission of a crime, a punishment is inflicted, the more just and useful it will be. It will be more just, because it spares the criminal the cruel and superfluous torment of uncertainty, which increases in proportion to the strength of his imagination and the sense of his weakness; and because the privation of liberty, being a punishment, ought to be inflicted before condemnation, but for as short a time as possible. Imprisonments, I say, being only the means of securing the person of the accused, until he be tried, condemned or acquitted, ought not only to be of short duration, but attended with as little severity as possible. The time should be determined by the necessary preparation for the trial, and the right of priority in the oldest prisoners. The confinement ought not to be closer than is requisite to prevent his flight, or his concealing the proofs of the crime; and the trial should be conducted with all possible expedition. Can there be a more cruel contrast than that between the indolence of a judge, and the painful anxiety of the accused; the comforts and pleasures of an insensible magistrate, and the filth and misery of the prisoner? In general, as I have before observed, *The degree of the punishment, and the consequences of a crime, ought to be so contrived, as to have the greatest possible effect on others, with the least possible pain to the delinquent.* If there be any society in which this is not a fundamental principle, it is an unlawful society; for mankind, by their union, originally intended to subject themselves to the least evils possible.

An immediate punishment is more useful; because the smaller the interval of time between the punishment and the crime, the stronger and more lasting will be the association of the two ideas of *Crime* and *Punishment:* so that they may be considered, one as the cause, and the other as the unavoidable and necessary effect. It is demonstrated, that the association of ideas is the cement which unites the fabric of the human intellect; without which, pleasure and pain would be simple and ineffectual sensations. The vulgar, that is, all men who have no general ideas or universal principles, act in consequence of the most immediate and familiar associations; but the more remote and complex only present themselves to the minds of those who are passionately attached to a single object, or to those of greater understanding, who have acquired an habit of rapidly comparing together a number of objects, and of forming a conclusion; and the result, that is, the action, in consequence, by these means, becomes less dangerous and uncertain.

It is, then, of the greatest importance, that the punishment should succeed the crime, as immediately as possible, if we intend, that, in the rude minds of the multitude, the seducing picture of the advantage arising from the crime, should instantly awake the attendant idea of punishment. Delaying the punishment serves only to separate these two ideas; and thus affects the minds of the spectators rather as being a terrible sight than the necessary consequence of a crime; the horror of which should contribute to heighten the idea of the punishment.

There is another excellent method of strengthening this important connection between the ideas of crime and punishment; that is, to make the punishment as analagous as possible to the nature of the crime; in order that the punishment may lead the mind to consider the crime in a different point of view, from that in which it was placed by the flattering idea of promised advantages.

Crimes of less importance are commonly punished, either in the obscurity of a prison, or the criminal is *transported,* to give, by his slavery, an example to societies which he never offended; an example absolutely useless, because distant from the place where the crime was committed. Men do not, in general, commit great crimes deliberately, but rather in a sudden gust of passion; and they commonly look on the punishment due to a great crime as remote and improbable. The public punishment,

therefore, of small crimes will make a greater impression, and, by deterring men from the smaller,
will effectually prevent the greater.

OF ACTS OF VIOLENCE.

SOME crimes relate to *person*, others to *property.* The first ought to be punished corporally. The great and rich should by no means have it in their power to set a price on the security of the weak and indigent; for then, riches, which, under the protection of the laws, are the reward of industry, would become the aliment of tyranny. Liberty is at an end, whenever the laws permit, that, in certain cases, a man may cease to be a *person,* and become a *thing.* Then will the powerful employ their address to select from the various combinations of civil society, all that is in their own favour. This is that magic art which transforms subjects into beasts of burden, and which, in the hands of the strong, is the chain that binds the the weak and incautious. Thus it is, that in some governments, where there is all the appearance of liberty, tyranny lies concealed, and insinuates itself into some neglected corner of the constitution, where it gathers strength insensibly. Mankind generally oppose, with resolution, the assaults of barefaced and open tyranny; but disregard the little insect that gnaws through the dyke, and opens a sure, though secret, passage to inundation.

OF THE PUNISHMENT OF THE NOBLES.

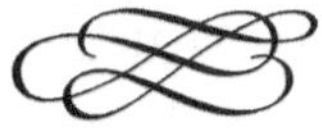

WHAT punishments shall be ordained for the nobles, whose privileges make so great a part of the laws of nations? I do not mean to inquire whether the hereditary distinction between nobles and commoners be useful in any government, or necessary in a monarchy; or whether it be true, that they form an intermediate power, of use in moderating the excesses of both extremes; or whether they be not rather slaves to their own body, and to others, confining within a very small circle the natural effects and hopes of industry, like those little fruitful spots scattered here and there in the sandy deserts of Arabia; or whether it be true that a subordination of rank and condition is inevitable, or useful in society; and if so, whether this subordination should not rather subsist between individuals than particular bodies; whether it should not rather circulate through the whole body

politic, than be confined to one part; and rather than
be perpetual, should it not be incessantly produced
and destroyed. Be these as they may, I assert that
the punishment of a nobleman should in no wise
differ from that of the lowest member of society.

Every lawful distinction, either in honours or
riches, supposes previous equality, founded on the
laws, on which all the members of society are considered as being equally dependent. We should suppose that men, in renouncing their natural
despotism, said, *the wisest and most industrious
among us shall obtain the greatest honours, and his dignity shall descend to his posterity. The fortunate and
happy may hope for greater honours, but let him not
therefore be less afraid than others of violating those conditions on which he is exalted.* It is true, indeed, that
no such decrees were ever made in a general diet of
mankind, but they exist in the invariable relations of
things: nor do they destroy the advantages which
are supposed to be produced by the class of nobles,
but prevent the inconveniencies; and they make the
laws respectable by destroying all hopes of
impunity.

It may be objected, that the same punishment
inflicted on a nobleman and a plebeian, becomes really different from the difference of their education
and from the infamy it reflects on an illustrious family; but I answer, that punishments are to be estimated, not by the sensibility of the criminal, but by
the injury done to society; which injury is aug-
mented by the high rank of the offender. The precise
equality of a punishment can never be more than
external, as it is in proportion to the degree of sensi-

bility, which differs in every individual. The infamy of an innocent family may be easily obliterated by some public demonstration of favour from the sovereign; and forms have always more influence than reason on the gazing multitude.

OF ROBBERY.

THE punishment of robbery, not accompanied with violence, should be pecuniary. He who endeavours to enrich himself with the property of another, should be deprived of part of his own. But this crime, alas! is commonly the effect of misery and despair; the crime of that unhappy part of mankind, to whom the right of exclusive property, a terrible, and perhaps unnecessary right, has left but a bare existence. Besides, as pecuniary punishment may increase the number of poor, and may deprive an innocent family of subsistence, the most proper punishment will be that kind of slavery, which alone can be called just; that is, which makes the society, for a time, absolute master of the person and labour of the criminal, in order to oblige him to repair, by this dependence, the unjust despotism he usurped over the property of another, and his violation of the social compact.

When robbery is attended with violence, corporal punishment should be added to slavery. Many writers have shown the evident disorder which must arise from not distinguishing the punishment due to robbery with violence, and that due to theft, or robbery committed with dexterity, absurdly making a sum of money equivalent to a man's life. But it can never be superfluous to repeat, again and again, those truths of which mankind have not profited; for political machines preserve their motion much longer than others, and receive a new impulse with more difficulty. These crimes are in their nature absolutely different, and this axiom is as certain in politics as in mathematics, that between qualities of different natures there can be no similitude.

OF INFAMY, CONSIDERED AS A PUNISHMENT.

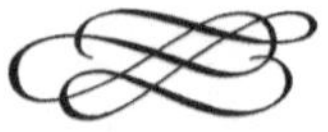

THOSE injuries, which affect the honour, that is, that just portion of esteem which every citizen has a right to expect from others, should be punished with infamy. Infamy is a mark of the public disapprobation, which deprives the object of all consideration in the eyes of his fellow citizens, of the confidence of his country, and of that fraternity which exists between members of the same society. This is not always in the power of the laws. It is necessary that the infamy inflicted by the laws should be the same with that which results from the relations of things, from universal morality, or from that particular system, adopted by the nation and the laws, which governs the opinion of the vulgar. If, on the contrary, one be different from the other, either the laws will no longer be respected, or the received notions of morality and probity will vanish in spite of the declamations of moralists, which are weak to resist the force of example. If we declare those actions infamous, which are in themselves indifferent, we lessen the infamy of those which are really infamous.

The punishment of infamy should not be too frequent, for the power of opinion grows weaker by repetition; nor should it be inflicted on a number of persons at the same time, for the infamy of many resolves itself into the infamy of none.

Painful and corporal punishments should never be applied to fanaticism; for being founded on pride, it glories in persecution. Infamy and ridicule only should be employed against fanatics; if the first, their pride will be overbalanced by the pride of the people; and we may judge of the power of the second, if we consider that even truth is obliged to summon all her force, when attacked by error armed with ridicule. Thus, by opposing one passion to another, and opinion to opinion, a wise legislator puts an end to the admiration of the populace, occasioned by a false principle, the original absurdity of which is veiled by some well-deduced consequences.

This is the method to avoid confounding the immutable relations of things, or opposing nature, whose actions not being limited by time, but operating incessantly, overturn and destroy all those vain regulations which contradict her laws. It is not only in the fine arts that the imitation of nature is the fundamental principle; it is the same in sound policy, which is no other than the art of uniting, and directing to the same end, the natural and immutable sentiments of mankind.

OF IDLENESS.

A WISE government will not suffer, in the midst of labour and industry, that kind of political idleness which is confounded, by rigid declaimers, with the leisure attending riches acquired by industry, which is of use to an increasing society, when confined within proper limits. I call those politically idle, who neither contribute to the good of society by their labour nor their riches; who continually accumulate, but never spend; and are reverenced by the vulgar with stupid admiration, and regarded by the wise with disdain; who, being victims to a monastic life, and deprived of all incitement to the activity which is necessary to preserve or increase its comforts, devote all their vigour to passions of the strongest kind, the passions of opinion. I call him not idle, who enjoys the fruits of the virtues or vices of his ancestors, and in exchange for his pleasures supports the industrious poor. It is not then the narrow virtue of austere moralists, but the laws, that should determine what species of idleness deserves punishment.

OF BANISHMENT, AND CONFISCATION.

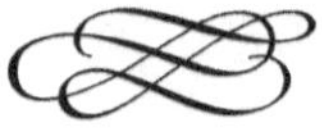

HE who disturbs the public tranquillity, who does not obey the laws, who violates the conditions on which men mutually support and defend each other, ought to be excluded from society, that is, banished.

It seems as if banishment should be the punishment of those, who, being accused of an atrocious crime, are probably, but not certainly, guilty. For this purpose would be required a law, the least arbitrary, and the most precise possible; which should condemn to banishment those who have reduced the community to the fatal alternative, either of fearing or punishing them unjustly; still, however, leaving them the sacred right of proving their innocence. The reasons ought to be stronger for banishing a citizen than a stranger, and for the first accusation than for one who hath been often excused.

Should the person who is excluded for ever from society be deprived of his property? This question may be considered in different lights. The confiscation of effects, added to banishment, is a greater punishment than banishment alone; there ought then to be some cases, in which, according to the crime, either the whole fortune should be confiscated, or part only, or none at all. The whole should be forfeited, when the law, which ordains banishment, declares, at the same time, that all connections between the society and the criminal are annihilated. In this case, the citizen dies, the man only remains; and with respect to a political body, the death of the *citizen* should have the same consequences with the death of the *man*. It seems to follow, then, that in this case, the effects of the criminal should devolve to his lawful heirs. But it is not on account of this refinement that I disapprove of confiscations. If some have insisted that they were a restraint to vengeance, and the violence of particulars, they have not reflected, that though punishments be productive of good, they are not, on that account, more just; to be just, they must be necessary. Even an useful injustice can never be allowed by a legislator, who means to guard against watchful tyranny; which, under the flattering pretext of momentary advantages, would establish permanent principles of destruction, and, to procure the ease of a few in a high station, would draw tears from thousands of the poor.

The law which ordains confiscations, sets a price on the head of the subject, with the guilty punishes the innocent, and by reducing them to indigence and despair, tempts them to become criminal. Can there be a more melancholy spectacle, than a whole family, overwhelmed with infamy and misery, from the crime of their chief? a crime, which if it had been possible, they were restrained from preventing, by that submission which the laws themselves have ordained.

OF THE SPIRIT OF FAMILY IN STATES.

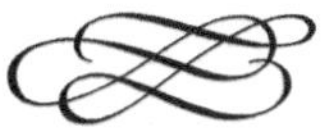

IT is remarkable, that many fatal acts of injustice have been authorised and approved, even by the wisest and most experienced men, in the freest republics. This has been owing to their having considered the state, rather as a society of *families,* than of *men.* Let us suppose a nation, composed of an hundred thousand men, divided into twenty thousand families of five persons each, including the head or master of the family, its representative. If it be an association of *families,* there will be twenty thousand *men,* and eighty thousand slaves; if of *men,* there will be an hundred thousand citizens, and not one slave. In the first case we behold a republic, and twenty thousand little monarchies, of which the heads are the sovereigns; in the second, the spirit of liberty will not only breathe in every public place of the city, and in the assemblies of the nation, but in private houses, where men find the greatest part of their happiness or misery. As laws and customs are always the effect of a republic, if the society be an association of the heads of families, the spirit of monarchy will gradually make its way into the republic itself, as its effects will only be restrained by the opposite interests of each; and not by an universal spirit of liberty and equality. The private spirit of family is a spirit of minuteness, and confined to little concerns. Public spirit, on the contrary, is influenced by general principles, and from facts deduces general rules of utility to the greatest number.

In a republic of families, the children remain under the authority of the father, as long as he lives, and are obliged to wait until death for an existence dependent on the laws alone. Accustomed to kneel and tremble in their tender years, when their natural sentiments were less restrained by that caution, obtained by experience, which is called moderation, how should they resist those obstacles, which vice always opposes to virtue, in the languor and decline of age, when the despair of reaping the fruits is alone sufficient to damp the vigour of their resolutions.

In a republic, where every man is a citizen, family subordination is not the effect of compulsion, but of contract; and the sons, disengaged from the natural dependence, which the weakness of infancy and the necessity of education required, become free members of society, but remain subject to the head of the family for their own advantage, as in the great society.

In a republic of families, the young people, that is, the most numerous and most useful part of the nation, are at the discretion of their fathers: in a republic of men, they are attached to their parents by no other obligation, than that sacred and inviolable one of mutual assistance, and of gratitude for the benefits they have received; a sentiment, destroyed not so much by the wickedness of the human heart, as by a mistaken subjection, prescribed by the laws.

These contradictions between the laws of families, and the fundamental laws of a state, are the source of many others between public and private morality, which produce a perpetual conflict in the mind. Domestic morality inspires submission and fear: the other, courage and liberty. That instructs a man to confine his beneficence to a small number of persons, not of his own choice; this, to extend it to all mankind: that commands a continual sacrifice of himself to a vain idol, called the *good of the family,* which is often no real good to any one of those who compose it; this teaches him to consider his own advanatge without offending the laws, or excites him to sacrifice himself for the good of his country by rewarding him beforehand with the fanaticism it inspires. Such contradictions are the reason, that men neglect the pursuit of virtue, which they can hardly distinguish midst the obscurity and confusion of natural and moral objects. How frequently are men, upon a retrospection of their actions, astonished to find themselves dishonest.

In proportion to the increase of society, each member becomes a smaller part of the whole; and the republican spirit diminishes in the same proportion, if neglected by the laws. Political societies, like the human body, have their limits circumscribed, which they cannot exceed without disturbing their economy. It seems as if the greatness of a state ought to be inversely as the sensibility and activity of the individuals; if, on the contrary, population and inactivity increase in the same proportion, the laws will with difficulty prevent the crimes arising from the good they have produced. An overgrown republic can only be saved from despotism, by subdividing it into a number of confederate republics. But how is this practicable? By a despotic dictator, who, with the courage of *Sylla,* has as much genius for building up, as that Roman had for pulling down. If he be an ambitious man, his reward will be immortal glory; if a philosopher, the blessings of his fellow citizens will sufficiently console him for the loss of authority, though he should not be insensible to their ingratitude.

In proportion as the sentiments, which unite us to the state, grow weaker, those which attach us to the objects which more immediately surround us grow stronger; therefore, in the most despotic government, friendships are more durable, and domestic virtues (which are always of the lowest class) are the most common, or the only virtues existing. Hence it appears how confined have been the views of the greatest number of legislators.

OF THE MILDNESS OF PUNISHMENTS.

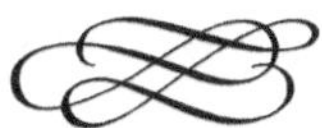

THE course of my ideas has carried me away from my subject, to the elucidation of which I now return. Crimes are more effectually prevented by the *certainty,* than the *severity* of punishment. Hence, in a magistrate, the necessity of vigilance, and, in a judge, of implacability, which, that it may become an useful virtue, should be joined to a mild legislation. The certainty of a small punishment will make a stronger impression, than the fear of one more severe, if attended with the hopes of escaping; for it is the nature of mankind to be terrified at the approach of the smallest inevitable evil, whilst hope, the best gift of Heaven, hath the power of dispelling the apprehension of a greater; especially if supported by examples of impunity, which weakness or avarice too frequently afford.

If punishments be very severe, men are naturally led to the perpetration of other crimes, to avoid the punishment due to the first. The countries and times most notorious for severity of punishments, were always those in which the most bloody and inhuman actions and the most atrocious crimes were committed; for the hand of the legislator and the assassin were directed by the same spirit of ferocity: which on the throne, dictated laws of iron to slaves and savages, and in private instigated the subject to sacrifice one tyrant, to make room for another.

In proportion as punishments become more cruel, the minds of men, as a fluid rises to the same height with that which surrounds it, grow hardened and insensible; and the force of passions still continuing, in the space of an hundred years, the *wheel* terrifies no more than formerly the *prison*. That a punishment may produce the effect required, it is sufficient that the *evil* it occasions should exceed the *good* expected from the crime; including in the calculation the certainty of the punishment, and the privation of the expected advantage. All severity beyond this is superfluous, and therefore tyrannical.

Men regulate their conduct by the repeated impression of evils they know, and not by those with which they are unacquainted. Let us, for example, suppose two nations, in one of which the greatest punishment is *perpetual slavery,* and in the other *the wheel.* I say, that both will inspire the same degree of terror; and that there can be no reasons for increasing the punishments of the first, which are not equally valid for augmenting those of the second to more lasting and more ingenious modes of tormenting; and so on to the most exquisite refinements of a science too well known to tyrants.

There are yet two other consequences of cruel punishments, which counteract the purpose of their institution, which was, to prevent crimes. The *first* arises from the impossibility of establishing an exact proportion between the crime and punishment; for though ingenious cruelty hath greatly multiplied the variety of torments, yet the human frame can suffer only to a certain degree, beyond which it is impossible to proceed, be the enormity of the crime ever so great. The *second* consequence is impunity. Human nature is limited no less in evil than in good. Excessive barbarity can never be more than temporary; it being impossible that it should be supported by a permanent system of legislation; for if the laws be too cruel, they must be altered, or anarchy and impunity will succeed.

Is it possible, without shuddering with horror, to read in history of the barbarous and useless torments that were coolly invented and executed by men who were called sages? Who does not tremble at the thoughts of thousands of wretches, whom their misery, either caused or tolerated by the laws which favoured the few and outraged the many, had forced in despair to return to a state of nature; or accused of impossible crimes, the fabric of ignorance and superstition; or guilty only of having been faithful to their own principles; who, I say, can, without horror, think of their being torn to pieces with slow and studied barbarity, by men endowed with the same passions and the same feelings? A delightful spectacle to a fanatic multitude!

OF THE PUNISHMENT OF DEATH.

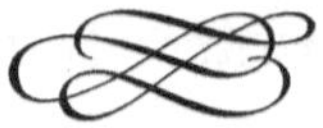

THE useless profusion of punishments, which has never made men better, induces me to inquire, whether the punishment of *death* be really just or useful in a well-governed state? What *right,* I ask, have men to cut the throats of their fellow-creatures? Certainly not that on which the sovereignty and laws are founded. The laws, as I have said before, are only the sum of the smallest portions of the private liberty of each individual, and represent the general will, which is the aggregate of that of each individual. Did any one ever give to others the right of taking away his life? Is it possible, that in the smallest portions of the liberty of each, sacrificed to the good of the public, can be obtained the greatest of all good, life? If it were so, how shall it be reconciled to the maxim which tells us, that a man has no right to kill himself? Which he certainly must have, if he could give it away to another.

But the punishment of death is not authorised by any right; for I have demonstrated that no such right exists. It is therefore a war of a whole nation against a citizen, whose destruction they consider as necessary or useful to the general good. But if I can further demonstrate, that it is neither necessary nor useful, I shall have gained the cause of humanity.

The death of a citizen cannot be necessary but in one case. When, though deprived of his liberty, he has such power and connections as may endanger the security of the nation; when his existence may produce a dangerous revolution in the established form of government. But even in this case, it can only be necessary when a nation is on the verge of recovering or losing its liberty; or in times of absolute anarchy, when the disorders themselves hold the place of laws. But in a reign of tranquillity; in a form of government approved by the united wishes of the nation; in a state fortified from enemies without, and supported by strength within, and opinion, perhaps more efficacious; where all power is lodged in the hands of the true sovereign; where riches can purchase pleasures and not authority, there can be no necessity for taking away the life of a subject.

If the experience of all ages be not sufficient to prove, that the punishment of death has never prevented determined men from injuring society; if the example of the Romans; if twenty years reign of Elizabeth, empress of Russia, in which she gave the fathers of their country an example more illustrious than many conquests bought with blood; if, I say, all this be not sufficient to persuade mankind, who always suspect the voice of reason, and who choose rather to be led by authority, let us consult human nature in proof of my assertion.

It is not the intenseness of the pain that has the greatest effect on the mind, but its continuance; for our sensibility is more easily and more powerfully affected by weak, but by repeated impressions, than by a violent but momentary impulse. The power of habit is universal over every sensible being. As it is by that we learn to speak, to walk, and to satisfy our necessities, so the ideas of morality are stamped on our minds by repeated impressions. The death of a criminal is a terrible but momentary spectacle, and therefore a less efficacious method of deterring others, than the continued example of a man deprived of his liberty, condemned as a beast of burden, to repair, by his labour, the injury he has done to society. *If I commit such a crime,* says the spectator to himself, *I shall be reduced to that miserable condition for the rest of my life.* A much more powerful preventive than the fear of death, which men always behold in distant obscurity.

The terrors of death make so slight an impression, that it has not force enough to withstand the forgetfulness natural to mankind, even in the most essential things; especially when assisted by the passions. Violent impressions surprise us, but their effect is momentary; they are fit to produce those revolutions which instantly transform a common man into a Lacedæmonian or a Persian; but in a free and quiet government they ought to be rather frequent than strong.

The execution of a criminal is, to the multitude, a

spectacle which in some excites compassion mixed with indignation. These sentiments occupy the mind much more than that salutary terror which the laws endeavour to inspire; but in the contemplation of continued suffering, terror is the only, or at least, the predominant sensation. The severity of a punishment should be just sufficient to excite compassion in the spectators, as it is intended more for them than for the criminal.

A punishment, to be just, should have only that degree of severity which is sufficient to deter others. Now there is no man, who, upon the least reflection, would put in competition the total and perpetual loss of his liberty, with the greatest advantages he could possibly obtain in consequence of a crime. Perpetual slavery, then, has in it all that is necessary to deter the most hardened and determined, as much as the punishment of death. I say, it has more. There are many who can look upon death with intrepidity and firmness; some through fanaticism, and others through vanity, which attends us even to the grave; others from a desperate resolution, either to get rid of their misery, or cease to live: but fanaticism and vanity forsake the criminal in slavery, in chains and fetters, in an iron cage; and despair seems rather the beginning than the end of their misery. The mind, by collecting itself and uniting all its force, can, for a moment, repel assailing grief; but its most vigorous efforts are insufficient to resist perpetual wretchedness.

In all nations, where death is used as punishment, every example supposes a new crime committed. Whereas, in perpetual slavery, every criminal affords a frequent and lasting example: and if it be necessary that men should often be witnesses of the power of the laws, criminals should often be put to death; but this supposes a frequency of crimes; and from hence this punishment will cease to have its effect, so that it must be useful and useless at the same time.

I shall be told, that perpetual slavery is as painful a punishment as death, and therefore as cruel. I answer, that if all the miserable moments in the life of a slave were collected into one point, it would be a more cruel punishment than any other; but these are scattered through his whole life, whilst the pain of death exerts all its force in a moment. There is also another advantage in the punishment of slavery, which is, that it is more terrible to the spectator than to the sufferer himself; for the spectator considers the sum of all his wretched moments, whilst the sufferer, by the misery of the present, is prevented from thinking of the future. All evils are increased by the imagination, and the sufferer finds resources and consolation, of which the spectators are ignorant; who judge by their own sensibility of what passes in a mind by habit grown callous to misfortune.

Let us, for a moment, attend to the reasoning of a robber or assassin, who is deterred from violating the laws by the gibbet or the wheel. I am sensible, that to develop the sentiments of one's own heart, is an art which education only can teach; but although a villain may not be able to give a clear account of his principles, they nevertheless influence his conduct. He reasons thus: "What are these laws that I am bound to respect, which make so great a difference between me and the rich man? He refuses me the farthing I ask of him, and excuses himself by bidding me have recourse to labour, with which he is unacquainted. Who made these laws? The rich and the great, who never deigned to visit the miserable hut of the poor; who have never seen him dividing a piece of mouldy bread, amidst the cries of his famished children, and the tears of his wife. Let us break those ties, fatal to the greatest part of mankind, and only useful to a few indolent tyrants. Let us attack injustice at its source. I will return to my natural state of independence. I shall live free and happy on the fruits of my courage and industry. A day of pain and repentance may come, but it will be short; and for an hour of grief, I shall enjoy years of pleasure and liberty. King of a small number, as determined as myself, I will correct the mistakes of fortune; and shall see those tyrants grow pale and tremble at the sight of him, whom, with insulting pride, they would not suffer to rank with dogs and horses."

Religion then presents itself to the mind of this lawless villain, and promising him almost a certainty of eternal happiness upon the easy terms of repentance, contributes much to lessen the horror of the last scene of the tragedy.

But he who foresees that he must pass a great number of years, even his whole life, in pain and slavery; a slave to those laws by which he was protected; in sight of his fellow citizens, with whom he lives in freedom and society; makes an useful comparison between those evils, the uncertainty of his success, and the shortness of the time in which he shall enjoy the fruits of his transgression. The example of those wretches continually before his eyes, makes a much greater impression on him than a punishment, which, instead of correcting, makes him more obdurate.

The punishment of death is pernicious to society, from the example of barbarity it affords. If the passions, or necessity of war, have taught men to shed the blood of their fellow creatures, the laws which are intended to moderate the ferocity of mankind, should not increase it by examples of barbarity, the more horrible, as this punishment is usually attended with formal pageantry. Is it not absurd, that the laws, which detect and punish homicide, should, in order to prevent murder, publicly commit murder themselves? What are the true and most useful laws? Those compacts and conditions which all would propose and observe, in those moments when private interest is silent, or combined with that of the public. What are the natural sentiments of every person concerning the punishment of death? We may read them in the contempt and indignation with which every one looks on the executioner, who is nevertheless an innocent executor of the public will; a good citizen, who contributes to the advantage of society; the instrument of the general security within, as good soldiers are without. What then is the origin of this contradiction? Why is this sentiment of mankind indelible to the scandal of reason? It is, that in a secret corner of the mind, in which the original impressions of nature are still preserved, men discover a sentiment which tells them, that their lives are not lawfully in the power of any one, but of that necessity only, which with its iron sceptre rules the universe.

What must men think, when they see wise magistrates and grave ministers of justice, with indifference and tranquillity, dragging a criminal to death, and whilst a wretch trembles with agony, expecting the fatal stroke, the judge, who has condemned him, with the coldest insensibility, and perhaps with no small gratification from the exertion of his authority, quits his tribunal to enjoy the comforts and pleasures of life? They will say, "Ah! those cruel formalities of justice are a cloak to tyranny, they are a secret language, a solemn veil, intended to conceal the sword by which we are sacrificed to the insatiable idol of despotism. Murder, which they would represent to us as an horrible crime, we see practiced by them without repugnance or remorse. Let us follow their example. A violent death appeared terrible in their descriptions, but we see that it is the affair of a moment. It will be still less terrible to him, who, not expecting it, escapes almost all the pain." Such is the fatal, though absurd reasoning of men who are disposed to commit crimes; on whom the abuse of religion has more influence than religion itself.

If it be objected, that almost all nations in all ages have punished certain crimes with death, I answer that the force of these examples vanishes, when opposed to truth, against which prescription is urged in vain. The history of mankind is an immense sea of errors, in which a few obscure truths may here and there be found.

But human sacrifices have also been common in almost all nations. That some societies only, either few in number, or for a very short time, abstained from the punishment of death, is rather favourable to my argument, for such is the fate of great truths, that their duration is only as a flash of lightning in the long and dark night of error. The happy time is not yet arrived, when truth, as falsehood has been hitherto, shall be the portion of the greatest number.

I am sensible that the voice of one philosopher is too weak to be heard amidst the clamours of a multitude, blindly influenced by custom; but there is a small number of sages, scattered on the face of the earth, who will echo to me from the bottom of their hearts; and if these truths should happily force their way to the thrones of princes, be it known to them, that they come attended with the secret wishes of all mankind, and tell the sovereign who deigns them a gracious reception, that his fame shall outshine the glory of conquerors, and that equitable posterity will exalt his peaceful trophies above those of a Titus, an Antoninus, or a Trajan.

How happy were mankind, if laws were now to be first formed! now that we see on the thrones of Europe benevolent monarchs, friends to the virtues of peace, to the arts and sciences, fathers of their people, though crowned yet citizens; the increase of whose authority augments the happiness of their subjects, by destroying that intermediate despotism which intercepts the prayers of the people to the throne. If these humane princes have suffered the old laws to subsist, it is doubtless because they are deterred by the numberless obstacles which oppose the subversion of errors established by the sanction of many ages; and therefore every wise citizen will wish for the increase of their authority.

OF IMPRISONMENT.

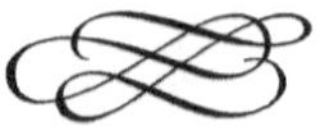

THAT a magistrate, the executor of the laws, should have a power to imprison a citizen, to deprive the man he hates of his liberty upon frivolous pretences, and to leave his friend unpunished, notwithstanding the strongest proofs of his guilt, is an error as common as it is contrary to the end of society, which is personal security.

Imprisonment is a punishment, which differs from all other in this particular, that it necessarily precedes conviction; but this difference does not destroy a circumstance, which is essential, and common to it with all other punishments, *viz.* that it should never be inflicted, but when ordained by the law. The law should, therefore, determine the crime, the presumption, and the evidence sufficient to subject the accused to imprisonment and examination. Public report, his flight, his extra-judicial confession, that of an accomplice, menaces, and his constant enmity with the person injured, the circumstances of the crime, and such other evidence, may be sufficient to justify the imprisonment of a citizen. But the nature of this evidence should be determined by the laws, and not by the magistrates, whose decrees are always contrary to political liberty, when they are not particular applications of a general maxim of the public code. When punishments become less severe, and prisons less horrible; when compassion and humanity shall penetrate the iron gates of dungeons, and direct the obdurate and inexorable ministers of justice, the laws may then be satisfied with weaker evidence for imprisonment.

A person accused, imprisoned, tried and acquitted, ought not to be branded with any degree of infamy. Among the Romans, we see that many, accused of very great crimes, and afterwards declared innocent, were respected by the people, and honoured with employments in the state. But why is the fate of an innocent person so different in this age? It is, because the present system of penal laws presents to our minds an idea of power rather than of justice. It is, because the accused and convicted are thrown indiscriminately into the same prison; because imprisonment is rather a punishment, than a means of securing the person of the accused; and because the interior power, which defends the laws, and the exterior, which defends the throne and kingdom, are separate when they should be united. If the first were (under the common authority of the laws) combined with the right of judging, but not, however immediately dependent on the magistrate, the pomp that attends a military corps, would take off the infamy; which, like all popular opinions, is more attached to the manner and form, than to the thing itself; as may be seen in military imprisonment, which, in the common opinion, is not so disgraceful as the civil. But the barbarity and ferocity of our ancestors, the hunters of the north, still subsist among the people, in our customs and our laws, which are always several ages behind the actual refinements of a nation.

OF PROSECUTION AND PRESCRIPTION.

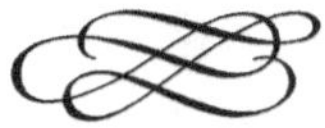

THE proofs of the crime being obtained, and the certainty of it determined, it is necessary to allow the criminal the time and means for his justification; but a time so short, as not to diminish that promptitude of punishment, which, as we have shown, is one of the most powerful means of preventing crimes. A mistaken humanity may object to the shortness of the time, but the force of the objection will vanish, if we consider that the danger of the innocent increases with the defects of the legislation.

The time for inquiry and for justification should be fixed by the laws, and not by the judge, who, in that case, would become legislator. With regard to atrocious crimes, which are long remembered, when they are once proved, if the criminal have fled, no time should be allowed; but in less considerable and more obscure crimes, a time should be fixed, after which the delinquent should be no longer uncertain of his fate. For in the latter case, the length of time, in which the crime is almost forgotten, prevents the example of impunity, and allows the criminal to amend, and become a better member of society.

General principles will here be sufficient, it being impossible to fix precisely the limits of time for any given legislation, or for any society in any particular circumstance. I shall only add, that in a nation willing to prove the utility of moderate punishment, laws which, according to the nature of the crime increase or diminish the time of inquiry and justification, considering the imprisonment or the voluntary exile of the criminal as a part of the punishment, will form an easy division of a small number of mild punishments for a great number of crimes.

But, it must be observed, the time for inquiry and justification, should not increase in direct proportion to the atrociousness of crimes; for the probability of such crimes having been committed, is inversely as their atrociousness. Therefore the time for inquiring ought, in some cases, to be diminished, and that for justification increased, and *vice versa*. This may appear to contradict what I have said above, namely, that equal punishments may be decreed for unequal crimes, by considering the time allowed the criminal, or the prison, as a punishment.

In order to explain this idea, I shall divide crimes into two classes. The first comprehends homicide, and all greater crimes; the second, crimes of an inferior degree. This distinction is founded in human nature. The preservation of life is a natural right; the preservation of property is a right of society. The motives that induce men to shake off the natural sentiment of compassion, which must be destroyed before great crimes can be committed, are much less in number than those by which, from the natural desire of being happy, they are instigated to violate a right, which is not founded in the heart of man, but is the work of society. The different degrees of probability in these two classes, require that they should be regulated on different principles. In the greatest crimes, as they are less frequent, and the probability of the innocence of the accused being greater, the time allowed him for his justification should be greater, and the time of inquiry less. For by hastening the definitive sentence, the flattering hopes of impunity are destroyed, which are more dangerous, as the crime is more atrocious. On the contrary, in crimes of less importance, the probability of the innocence being less, the time of inquiry should be greater, and that of justification less, as impunity is not so dangerous.

But this division of crimes into two classes should not be admitted, if the consequences of impunity were in proportion to the probability of the crime. It should be considered, that a person accused, whose guilt or innocence is not determined for want of proofs, may be again imprisoned for the same crime, and be subject to a new trial, if fresh evidence arises within the time fixed.

This is, in my opinion, the best method of providing at the same time for the security and liberty of the subject, without favouring one at the expence

of the other; which may easily happen, since both
these blessings, the inalienable and equal patrimony
of every citizen, are liable to be invaded, the one by
open or disguised despotism, and the other by tumultuous and popular anarchy.

OF CRIMES OF DIFFICULT PROOF.

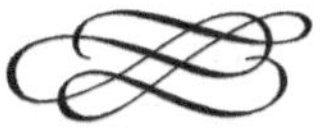

WITH the foregoing principles in view, it will appear astonishing, that reason hardly ever presided at the formation of the laws of nations; that the weakest and most equivocal evidence, and even conjectures, have been thought sufficient proof for crimes the most atrocious, (and therefore most improbable), the most obscure and chimerical; as if it were the interest of the laws and the judge not to inquire into the truth, but to prove the crime; as if there was not a greater risk of condemning an innocent person, when the probability of his guilt is less.

The generality of men want that vigour of mind and resolution, which are as necessary for great crimes as for great virtues, and which at the same time produce both the one and the other, in those nations which are supported by the activity of their government, and a passion for the public good. For in those which subsist by their greatness or power, or by the goodness of their laws, the passions being in a weaker degree, seem calculated rather to maintain than to improve the form of government. This naturally leads us to an important conclusion, *viz.* that great crimes do always produce the destruction of a nation.

There are some crimes which, though frequent in society, are of difficult proof, a circumstance admitted, as equal to the probability of the innocence of the accused. But as the frequency of these crimes is not owing to their impunity, so much as to other causes, the danger of their passing unpunished is of less importance, and therefore the time of examination and prescription may be equally diminished. These principles are different from those commonly received; for it is in crimes, which are proved with the greatest difficulty, such as adultery, and sodomy, that presumptions, half-proofs, etc. are admitted; as if a man could be half innocent, and half guilty; that is, half punishable and half absolvable. It is in these cases that torture should exercise its cruel power on the person of the accused, the witnesses, and even his whole family, as, with unfeeling indifference, some civilians have taught, who pretend to dictate laws to nations.

Adultery is a crime which, politically considered, owes its existence to two causes, *viz.* pernicious laws, and the powerful attraction between the sexes. This attraction is similar in many circumstances to gravity, the spring of motion in the universe. Like this, it is diminished by distance; one regulates the motions of the body, the other of the soul. But they differ in one respect; the force of gravity decreases in proportion to the obstacles that oppose it; the other gathers strength and vigour as the obstacles increase.

If I were speaking to nations guided only by the laws of nature, I would tell them, that there is a considerable difference between adultery and all other crimes. Adultery proceeds from an abuse of that necessity which is constant and universal in human nature; a necessity anterior to the formation of society, and indeed the founder of society itself; whereas, all other crimes tend to the destruction of society, and arise from momentary passions, and not from a natural necessity. It is the opinion of those, who have studied history and mankind, that this necessity is constantly in the same degree in the same climate. If this be true, useless, or rather pernicious must all laws and customs be, which tend to diminish the sum total of the effects of this passion. Such laws would only burden one part of the society with the additional necessities of the other; but, on the contrary, wise are the laws which, following the natural course of the river, divide the stream into a number of equal branches, preventing thus both sterility and inundation.

Conjugal fidelity is always greater in proportion as marriages are more numerous, and less difficult. But when the interest or pride of families, or paternal authority, not the inclination of the parties, unite the sexes, gallantry soon breaks the slender ties, in spite of common moralists, who exclaim against the effect, whilst they pardon the cause. But these reflections are useless to those, who, living in the true religion, act from sublimer motives, which correct the eternal laws of nature.

The act of adultery is a crime so instantaneous, so mysterious, and so concealed by the veil which the laws themselves have woven; a veil necessary indeed, but so transparent, as to heighten rather than conceal the charms of the object; the opportunities are so frequent, and the danger of discovery so easily avoided, that it were much easier for the laws to prevent this crime, than to punish it when committed.

To every crime, which from its nature must frequently remain unpunished, the punishment is an incentive. Such is the nature of the human mind, that difficulties, if not insurmountable, nor too great for our natural indolence, embellish the object, and spur us on to the pursuit. They are so many barriers that confine the imagination to the object, and oblige us to consider it in every point of view. In this agitation, the mind naturally inclines and fixes itself to the most agreeable part, studiously avoiding every idea that might create disgust.

The crime of sodomy, so severely punished by the laws, and for the proof of which are employed tortures, which often triumph over innocence itself, has its source much less in the passions of man in a free and independent state, than in society and a slave. It is much less the effect of a satiety in pleasures, than of that education, which, in order to make men useful to others, begins by making them useless to themselves. In those public seminaries, where ardent youth are carefully excluded from all commerce with the other sex, as the vigour of nature blooms, it is consumed in a manner not only useless to mankind, but which accelerates the approach of old age.

The murder of bastard children is, in like manner, the effect of a cruel dilemma, in which a woman finds herself who has been seduced through weakness, or overcome by force. The alternative is, her own infamy, or the death of a being who is incapable of feeling the loss of life. How can she avoid preferring the last to the inevitable misery of herself and her unhappy infant! The best method of preventing this crime, would be effectually to protect the weak woman from that tyranny which exaggerates all vices that cannot be concealed under the cloak of virtue.

I do not pretend to lessen that just abhorrence which these crimes deserve, but to discover the sources from whence they spring; and I think I may draw the following conclusions: *That the punishment of a crime cannot be just, (that is, necessary), if the laws have not endeavoured to prevent that crime by the best means which times and circumstances would allow.*

OF SUICIDE.

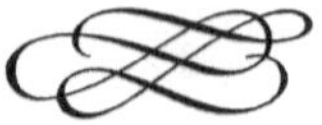

SUICIDE is a crime, which seems not to admit of punishment, properly speaking; for it cannot be inflicted but on the innocent, or upon an insensible dead body. In the first case, it is unjust and tyrannical, for political liberty supposes all punishments entirely personal; in the second, it has the same effect, by way of example, as the scourging a statue. Mankind love life too well; the objects that surround them; the seducing phantom of pleasure and hope, that sweetest error of mortals, which makes men swallow such large draughts of evil, mingled with a very few drops of good, allure them too strongly, to apprehend that this crime will ever be common from its unavoidable impunity. The laws are obeyed through fear of punishment, but death destroys all sensibility. What motive, then, can restrain the desperate hand of suicide?

He who kills himself does a less injury to society, than he who quits his country for ever; for the other leaves his property behind him, but this carries with him at least a part of his substance. Besides, as the strength of a society consists in the number of citizens, he who quits one nation to reside in another, becomes a double loss. This then is the question: whether it be advantageous to society, that its members should enjoy the unlimited privilege of migration?

Every law that is not armed with force, or which, from circumstances, must be ineffectual, should not be promulgated. Opinion, which reigns over the minds of men, obeys the slow and indirect impressions of the legislator, but resists them when violently and directly applied; and useless laws communicate their insignificance to the most salutary, which are regarded more as obstacles to be surmounted, than as safeguards of the public good. But further, our perceptions being limited, by enforcing the observance of laws which are evidently useless, we destroy the influence of the most salutary.

From this principle, a wise dispenser of public happiness may draw some useful consequences, the explanation of which would carry me too far from my subject, which is to prove the inutility of making the nation a prison. Such a law is vain, because, unless inaccessible rocks, or impassable seas, divide the country from all others, how will it be possible to secure every point of the circumference, or how will you guard the guards themselves? Besides, this crime, once committed, cannot be punished; and to punish it before hand, would be to punish the intention and not the action; the will, which is entirely out of the power of human laws. To punish the absent by confiscating his effects, besides the facility of collusion, which would inevitably be the case, and which, without tyranny, could not be prevented, would put a stop to all commerce with other nations. To punish the criminal when he returns, would be to prevent him from repairing the evil he had already done to society, by making his absence perpetual. Besides, any prohibition would increase the desire of removing, and would infallibly prevent strangers from settling in the country.

What must we think of a government which has no means, but fear, to keep its subjects in their own country; to which, by the first impressions of their infancy, they are so strongly attached. The most certain method of keeping men at home, is, to make them happy; and it is the interest of every state to turn the balance, not only of commerce, but of felicity in favour of its subjects. The pleasures of luxury are not the principal sources of this happiness; though, by preventing the too great accumulation of wealth in few hands, they become a necessary remedy against the too great inequality of individuals, which always increases with the progress of society.

When the populousness of a country does not increase in proportion to its extent, luxury favours despotism, for where men are most dispersed, there is least industry, the dependence of the poor upon the luxury of the rich is greatest, and the union of the oppressed against the oppressors is least to be feared. In such circumstances, rich and powerful men more easily command distinction, respect and service, by which they are raised to a greater height above the poor; for men are more independent the less they are observed, and are least observed when most numerous. On the contrary, when the number of people is too great in proportion to the extent of a country, luxury is a check to despotism; because it is a spur to industry, and because the labour of the poor affords so many pleasures to the rich, that they disregard the luxury of ostentation, which would remind the people of their dependence. Hence we see that in vast and depopulated states, the luxury of ostentation prevails over that of convenience; but, in the countries more populous, the luxury of convenience tends constantly to diminish the luxury of ostentation.

The pleasures of luxury have this inconvenience, that though they employ a great number of hands, yet they are only enjoyed by a few, whilst the rest, who do not partake of them, feel the want more sensibly, on comparing their state with that of others. Security and liberty, restrained by the laws, are the basis of happiness, and when attended by these, the pleasures of luxury favour population, without which they become the instrument of tyranny. As the most noble and generous animals fly to solitude and inaccessible deserts, and abandon the fertile plains to man, their greatest enemy; so men reject pleasure itself, when offered by the hand of tyranny.

But to return. If it be demonstrated, that the laws which imprison men in their own country are vain and unjust, it will be equally true of those which punish suicide, for that can only be punished after death, which is in the power of God alone; but it is

no crime, with regard to man, because the punishment falls on an innocent family. If it be objected,
that the consideration of such a punishment may
prevent the crime; I answer, that he who can calmly
renounce the pleasure of existence; who is so weary
of life as to brave the idea of eternal misery, will
never be influenced by the more distant and less
powerful considerations of family and children.

OF SMUGGLING.

SMUGGLING is a real offence against the
sovereign and the nation; but the punishment
should not brand the offender with infamy,
because this crime is not infamous in the public
opinion. By inflicting infamous punishments, for
crimes that are not reputed so, we destroy that idea
where it may be useful. If the same punishment be
decreed for killing a pheasant as for killing a man,
or for forgery, all difference between those crimes
will shortly vanish. It is thus that moral sentiments
are destroyed in the heart of man; sentiments, the
work of many ages and of much bloodshed; sentiments, that are so slowly, and with so much difficulty, produced, and for the establishment of which
such sublime motives, and such an apparatus of ceremonies, were thought necessary.

This crime is owing to the laws themselves; for
the higher the duties, the greater is the advantage,
and, consequently, the temptation; which tempta-

tion is increased by the facility of perpetration, when the circumference that is guarded is of great extent, and the merchandise prohibited is small in bulk. The seizure and loss of the goods attempted to be smuggled, together with those that are found along with them, is just; but it would be better to lessen the duty, because men risk only in proportion to the advantage expected.

This crime being a theft of what belongs to the prince, and consequently to the nation, why is it not attended with infamy? I answer, that crimes, which men consider as productive of no bad consequences to themselves, do not interest them sufficiently to excite their indignation. The generality of mankind, upon whom remote consequences make no impression, do not see the evil that may result from the practice of smuggling, especially if they reap from it any present advantage. They only perceive the loss sustained by the prince. They are not then interested in refusing their esteem to the smuggler, as to one who has committed a theft or a forgery, or other crimes, by which they themselves may suffer; from this evident principle, that a sensible being only interests himself in those evils with which he is acquainted.

Shall this crime, then, committed by one who has nothing to lose, go unpunished? No. There are certain species of smuggling, which so particularly affect the revenue, a part of government so essential, and managed with so much difficulty, that they deserve imprisonment, or even slavery; but yet of such a nature as to be proportioned to the crime. For example, it would be highly unjust that a smuggler of tobacco should suffer the same punishment with a robber or assassin; but it would be most conformable to the nature of the offence, that the produce of his labour should be applied to the use of the crown, which he intended to defraud.

OF BANKRUPTS.

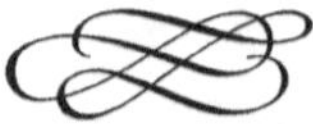

THE necessity of good faith in contracts and the support of commerce oblige the legislature to secure, for the creditors, the persons of bankrupts. It is, however, necessary to distinguish between the fraudulent and the honest bankrupt. The fraudulent bankrupt should be punished in the same manner with him who adulterates the coin; for to falsify a piece of coin, which is a pledge of the mutual obligation between citizens, is not a greater crime than to violate the obligations themselves. But the bankrupt who, after a strict examination, has proved before proper judges, that either the fraud or losses of others, or misfortunes unavoidable by human prudence, have stript him of his substance; upon what barbarous pretence is he thrown into prison, and deprived of the only remaining good, the melancholy enjoyment of mere liberty? Why is he ranked with criminals, and in despair compelled to repent of his honesty? Conscious of his innocence, he lived easy and happy under the protection of those laws, which it is true, he violated, but not intentionally. Laws, dictated by the avarice of the rich, and accepted by the poor, seduced by that universal flattering hope which makes men believe, that all unlucky accidents are the lot of others, and the most fortunate only their share. Mankind, when influenced by the first impressions, love cruel laws, although being subject to them themselves, it is the interest of every person that they should be as mild as possible; but the fear of being injured is always more prevalent than the intention of injuring others.

But to return to the honest bankrupt. Let his debt, if you will, not be considered as cancelled till the payment of the whole; let him be refused the liberty of leaving the country without leave of his creditors, or of carrying into another nation that industry which, under a penalty, he should be obliged to employ for their benefit; but what pretences can justify the depriving an innocent, though unfortunate man of his liberty, without the least utility to his creditors?

But, say they, the hardships of confinement will induce him to discover his fraudulent transactions; an event that can hardly be supposed, after a rigorous examination of his conduct and affairs. But if they are not discovered, he will escape unpunished. It is, I think, a maxim of government, that the importance of the political inconveniences, arising from the impunity of a crime, are directly as the injury to the public, and inversely as the difficulty of proof.

It will be necessary to distinguish fraud, attended with aggravating circumstances, from simple fraud, and that from perfect innocence. For the first, let there be ordained the same punishment as for forgery; for the second, a less punishment but with the loss of liberty; and if perfectly honest, let the bankrupt himself choose the method of re-establishing himself, and of satisfying his creditors; or if he should appear not to have been strictly honest, let that be determined by his creditors: but these distinctions should be fixed by the laws, which alone are impartial, and not by the arbitrary and dangerous prudence of judges.[1]

With what ease might a sagacious legislator prevent the greatest part of fraudulent bankruptcies, and remedy the misfortunes that befal the honest and industrious! A public register of all contracts, with the liberty of consulting it, allowed to every citizen; a public fund formed by a contribution of the opulent merchants for the timely assistance of unfortunate industry, were establishments that could produce no real inconveniences, and many advantages. But unhappily the most simple, the easiest, yet the wisest laws, that wait only for the nod of the legislator, to diffuse through nations wealth, power and felicity; laws which would be regarded by future generations with eternal gratitude, are either unknown or rejected. A restless and trifling spirit, the timid prudence of the present moment, a distrust and aversion to the most useful novelties, possess the minds of those who are empowered to regulate the actions of mankind.

1. It may be alledged, that the interest of commerce and property should be secured; but commerce and property are not the end of the social compact, but the means of obtaining that end; and to oppose all the members of society to cruel laws, to preserve them from evils, necessarily occasioned by the infinite combinations which result from the actual state of political societies, would be to make the end subservient to the means, a paralogism in all sciences, and particularly in politics. In the former editions of this work, I myself fell into this error, when I said that the honest bankrupt should be kept in custody, as a pledge for his debts, or employed as a slave to work for his creditors. I am ashamed of having adopted so cruel an opinion. I have been accused of impiety; I did not deserve it. I have been accused of sedition; I deserved it as little. But I insulted all the rights of humanity, and was never reproached.

OF SANCTUARIES.

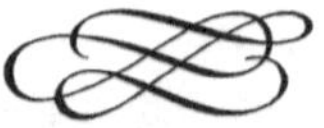

ARE sanctuaries just? Is a convention between nations, mutually to give up their criminals, useful?

In the whole extent of a political state, there should be no place independent of the laws. Their power should follow every subject, as the shadow follows the body. Sanctuaries, and impunity, differ only in degree, and as the effect of punishment depends more on their certainty, than their greatness, men are more strongly invited to crimes by sanctuaries, than they are deterred by punishment. To increase the number of sanctuaries, is to erect so many little sovereignties; for, when the laws have no power, new bodies will be formed in opposition to the public good, and a spirit established contrary to that of the state. History informs us, that from the use of sanctuaries have arisen the greatest revolutions in kingdoms and in opinions.

Some have pretended, that in whatever country

a crime, that is, an action contrary to the laws of society, be committed, the criminal may be justly punished for it in any other; as if the character of subject were indelible, or synonymous with, or worse than that of slave; as if a man could live in one country, and be subject to the laws of another, or be accountable for his actions to two sovereigns, or two codes of laws, often contradictory. There are also who think, that an act of cruelty committed, for example, at Constantinople may be punished at Paris; for this abstracted reason, that he who offends humanity, should have enemies in all mankind, and be the object of universal execration; as if judges were to be the knights-errant of human nature in general, rather than guardians of particular conventions between men. The place of punishment can certainly be no other, than that where the crime was committed; for the necessity of punishing an individual for the general good subsists there, and there only. A villain, if he has not broke through the conventions of a society of which, by my supposition, he was not a member, may be feared, and by force banished and excluded from that society; but ought not to be formally punished by the laws, which were only intended to maintain the social compact, and not to punish the intrinsic malignity of actions.

Whether it be useful that nations should mutually deliver up their criminals? Although the certainty of there being no part of the earth where crimes are not punished, may be a means of preventing them, I shall not pretend to determine this question, until, laws more conformable to the necessities and rights of humanity, and until milder punishments, and the abolition of the arbitrary power of opinion, shall afford security to virtue and innocence when oppressed; and until tyranny shall be confined to the plains of Asia, and Europe acknowledge the universal empire of reason, by which the interests of sovereigns and subjects are best united.

OF REWARDS FOR APPREHENDING, OR KILLING CRIMINALS.

LET us now inquire, whether it be advantageous to society, to set a price on the head of a criminal, and so to make of every citizen an executioner. If the offender hath taken refuge in another state, the sovereign encourages his subjects to commit a crime, and to expose themselves to a just punishment; he insults that nation, and authorises the subjects to commit on their neighbours similar usurpations. If the criminal still remain in his own country, to set a price upon his head, is the strongest proof of the weakness of the government. He who has strength to defend himself, will not purchase the assistance of another. Besides, such an edict confounds all the ideas of virtue and morality, already too wavering in the mind of man. At one time treachery is punished by the laws, at another encouraged. With one hand the legislator strengthens the ties of kindred and friendship, and with the other rewards the violation of both. Always in contradiction with himself, now he invites the suspecting minds of men to mutual confidence, and now he plants distrust in every heart. To prevent one crime, he gives birth to a thousand. Such are the expedients of weak nations, whose laws are like temporary repairs to a tottering fabric. On the contrary, as a nation becomes more enlightened, honesty and mutual confidence become more necessary, and are daily tending to unite with sound policy. Artifice, cabal, and obscure and indirect actions are more easily discovered, and the interest of the whole is better secured against the passions of the individual.

Even the times of ignorance, when private virtue was encouraged by public morality, may afford instruction and example to more enlightened ages. But laws which reward treason, excite clandestine war, and mutual distrust, oppose that necessary union of morality and policy, which is the foundation of happiness and universal peace.

OF ATTEMPTS. ACCOMPLICES AND PARDON.

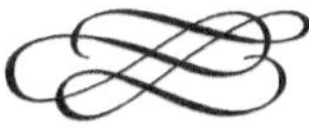

THE laws do not punish the intention; nevertheless an attempt which manifests the intention of committing a crime, deserves a punishment, though less, perhaps, than if the crime were actually perpetrated. The importance of preventing even attempts to commit a crime sufficiently authorises a punishment; but as there may be an interval of time between the attempt and the execution, it is proper to reserve the greater punishment for the actual commission, that even after the attempt there may be a motive for desisting.

In like manner, with regard to the accomplices, they ought not to suffer so severe a punishment as the immediate perpetrator of the crime. But this for a different reason. When a number of men unite, and run a common risk, the greater the danger, the more they endeavour to distribute it equally. Now, if the principals be punished more severely than the accessaries, it will prevent the danger from being equally divided, and will increase the difficulty of finding a person to execute the crime, as his danger is greater by the difference of the punishment. There can be but one exception to this rule; and that is, when the principal receives a reward from the accomplices. In that case, as the difference of the danger is compensated, the punishment should be equal. These reflections may appear too refined to those who do not consider, that it is of great importance, that the laws should leave the associates as few means as possible of agreeing among themselves.

In some tribunals, a pardon is offered to an accomplice in a great crime, if he discover his associates. This expedient has its advantages. The disadvantages are, that the law authorises treachery, which is detested even by the villains themselves; and introduces crimes of cowardice, which are much more pernicious to a nation than crimes of courage. Courage is not common, and only wants a benevolent power to direct it to the public good. Cowardice, on the contrary, is a frequent self-interested, and contagious evil, which can never be improved into a virtue. Besides, the tribunal, which has recourse to this method, betrays its fallibility, and the laws their weakness, by imploring the assistance of those by whom they are violated.

The advantages are, that it prevents great crimes, the effects of which being public, and the perpetrators concealed, terrify the people. It also contributes to prove, that he who violates the laws, which are public conventions, will also violate private compacts. It appears to me, that a general law, promising a reward to every accomplice who discovers his associates, would be better than a special declaration in every particular case; because it would prevent the union of those villains, as it would inspire a mutual distrust, and each would be afraid of exposing himself alone to danger. The accomplice, however, should be pardoned, on condition of transportation.

~

But it is in vain, that I torment myself with endeavouring to extinguish the remorse I feel in attempting to induce the sacred laws, the monument of public confidence, the foundation of human morality, to authorise dissimulation and perfidy. But what an example does it offer to a nation, to see the interpreters of the laws break their promise of pardon, and on the strength of learned subtleties, and to the scandal of public faith, drag him to punishment who hath accepted of their invitation! Such examples are not uncommon, and this is the reason, that political society is regarded as a complex machine, the springs of which are moved at pleasure by the most dexterous or most powerful.

OF SUGGESTIVE INTERROGATIONS.

THE laws forbid *suggestive interrogations;* that is, according to the civilians, questions which, with regard to the circumstances of the crime, are *special* when they should be *general;* or, in other words, those questions which, having an immediate reference to the crime, suggest to the criminal an immediate answer. Interrogations, according to the law, ought to lead to the fact indirectly and obliquely, but never directly or immediately. The intent of this injunction is, either that they should not suggest to the accused an immediate answer that might acquit him, or that they think it contrary to nature that a man should accuse himself. But whatever be the motive, the laws have fallen into a palpable contradiction, in condemning suggestive interrogations, whilst they authorise torture. Can there be an interrogation more suggestive than pain? Torture will suggest to a robust villain an obstinate silence, that he may exchange a greater punishment for a less; and to a feeble man confession, to relieve him from the present pain, which affects him more than the apprehension of the future. If a special interrogation be contrary to the right of nature, as it obliges a man to accuse himself, torture will certainly do it more effectually. But men are influenced more by the names than the nature of things.

He who obstinately refuses to answer the interrogatories, deserves a punishment, which should be fixed by the laws, and that of the severest kind; that criminals should not, by their silence, evade the example which they owe the public. But this punishment is not necessary when the guilt of the criminal is indisputable, because in that case interrogation is useless, as is likewise his confession, when there are, without it, proofs sufficient. This last case is most common, for experience shews, that in the greatest number of criminal prosecutions, the culprit pleads not guilty.

OF A PARTICULAR KIND OF CRIMES.

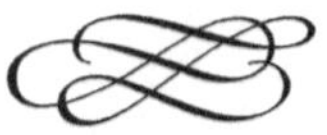

THE reader will perceive that I have omitted speaking of a certain class of crimes, which has covered Europe with blood, and raised up those horrid piles, from whence, midst clouds of whirling smoke, the groans of human victims, the crackling of their bones, and the frying of their still panting bowels, were a pleasing spectacle and agreeable harmony to the fanatic multitude. But men of understanding will perceive, that the age and country in which I live will not permit me to inquire into the nature of this crime. It were too tedious, and foreign to my subject, to prove the necessity of a perfect uniformity of opinions in a state, contrary to the examples of many nations; to prove that opinions, which differ from one another only in some subtile and obscure distinctions, beyond the reach of human capacity, may nevertheless disturb the public tranquillity, unless one only religion be established by authority; and that some opinions, by being contrasted and opposed to each other, in their collision strike out the truth; whilst others, feeble in themselves, require the support of power and authority. It would, I say, carry me too far, were I to prove, that, how odious soever is the empire of force over the opinions of mankind, from whom it only obtains dissimulation followed by contempt; and although it may seem contrary to the spirit of humanity and brotherly love, commanded us by reason, and authority, which we more respect, it is nevertheless necessary and indispensible. We are to believe, that all these paradoxes are resolved beyond a doubt, and are conformable to the true interest of mankind, if practised by a lawful authority. I write only of *crimes* which violate the laws of nature and the social contract, and not of *sins,* even the temporal punishments of which must be determined from other principles than those of a limited human philosophy.

OF FALSE IDEAS OF UTILITY.

A PRINCIPAL source of errors and injustice, are false ideas of utility. For example; that legislator has false ideas of utility, who considers particular more than general conveniences; who had rather command the sentiments of mankind than excite them, and dares say to reason, "Be thou a slave;" who would sacrifice a thousand real advantages to the fear of an imaginary or trifling inconvenience; who would deprive men of the use of fire for fear of being burnt, and of water for fear of their being drowned; and who know of no means of preventing evil, but by destroying it.

The laws of this nature, are those which forbid to wear arms, disarming those only who are not disposed to commit the crime which the laws mean to prevent. Can it be supposed, that those who have the courage to violate the most sacred laws of humanity, and the most important of the code, will respect the less considerable and arbitrary injunctions, the violation of which is so easy, and of so little comparative importance? Does not the execution of this law deprive the subject of that personal liberty, so dear to mankind and to the wise legislator; and does it not subject the innocent to all the disagreeable circumstances that should only fall on the guilty? It certainly makes the situation of the assaulted worse, and the assailants better, and rather encourages than prevents murder, as it requires less courage to attack armed than unarmed persons.

It is a false idea of utility, that would give to a multitude of sensible beings that symmetry and order, which inanimate matter is alone capable of receiving; to neglect the present, which are the only motives that act with force and constancy on the multitude, for the more distant, whose impressions are weak and transitory, unless increased by that strength of imagination so very uncommon among mankind. Finally, that is a false idea of utility, which, sacrificing things to names, separates the public good from that of individuals.

There is this difference between a state of society and a state of nature, that a savage does no more mischief to another than is necessary to procure some benefit to himself; but a man in society is sometimes tempted, from a fault in the laws, to injure another, without any prospect of advantage. The tyrant inspires his vassals with fear and servility, which rebound upon him with double force, and are the cause of his torment. Fear, the more private and domestic it is, the less dangerous is it to him who makes it the instrument of his happiness; but the more it is public, and the greater number of people it affects, the greater is the probability that some mad, desperate or designing person will seduce others to his party, by flattering expectations; and this will be the more easily accomplished, as the danger of the enterprise will be divided amongst a great number, because the value the unhappy set upon their existence is less, as their misery is greater.

OF THE MEANS OF PREVENTING CRIMES.

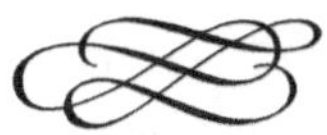

IT is better to prevent crimes than to punish them. This is the fundamental principle of good legislation, which is the art of conducting men to the *maximum* of happiness, and to the *minimum* of misery, if we may apply this mathematical expression to the good and evil of life. But the means hitherto employed for that purpose, are generally inadequate, or contrary to the end proposed. It is impossible to reduce the tumultuous activity of mankind to absolute regularity; for, midst the various and opposite attractions of pleasure and pain, human laws are not sufficient entirely to prevent disorders in society. Such, however, is the chimera of weak men, when invested with authority. To prohibit a number of indifferent actions, is not to prevent the crimes which they may produce, but to create new ones; it is to change at will the ideas of virtue and vice, which, at other times, we are told, are eternal and immutable. To what a situation should we be reduced, if every thing were to be forbidden that might possibly lead to a crime? We must be deprived of the use of our senses. For one motive that induces a man to commit a real crime, there are a thousand which excite him to those indifferent actions, which are called crimes by bad laws. If then, the probability that a crime will be committed be in proportion to the number of motives, to extend the sphere of crimes will be to increase that probability. The generality of laws are only exclusive privileges; the tribute of all to the advantage of a few.

Would you prevent crimes? Let the laws be clear and simple; let the entire force of the nation be united in their defence; let them be intended rather to favour every individual, than any particular classes of men; let the laws be feared, and the laws only. The fear of the laws is salutary, but the fear of men is a fruitful and fatal source of crimes. Men enslaved are more voluptuous, more debauched, and more cruel than those who are in a state of freedom. These study the sciences, the interest of nations, have great objects before their eyes, and imitate them; but those, whose views are confined to the present moment, endeavour, midst the distraction of riot and debauchery, to forget their situation; accustomed to the uncertainty of all events, for the laws determine none, the consequence of their crimes becomes problematical, which gives an additional force to the strength of their passions.

In a nation, indolent from the nature of the climate, the uncertainty of the laws confirms and increases men's indolence and stupidity. In a voluptuous but active nation, this uncertainty occasions a multiplicity of cabals and intrigues, which spread distrust and diffidence through the hearts of all, and dissimulation and treachery are the foundation of their prudence. In a brave and powerful nation, this uncertainty of the laws is at last destroyed, after many oscillations from liberty to slavery, and from slavery to liberty again.

OF THE SCIENCES.

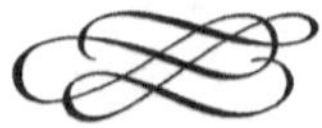

WOULD you prevent crimes? Let liberty be attended with knowledge. As knowledge extends, the disadvantages which attend it diminish, and the advantages increase. A daring impostor, who is always a man of some genius, is adored by the ignorant populace, and despised by men of understanding. Knowledge facilitates the comparison of objects, by shewing them in different points of view. When the clouds of ignorance are dispelled by the radiance of knowledge, authority trembles, but the force of the laws remains immoveable. Men of enlightened understanding must necessarily approve those useful conventions, which are the foundation of public safety; they compare, with the highest satisfaction, the inconsiderable portion of liberty of which they are deprived, with the sum total sacrificed by others for their security; observing that they have only given up the pernicious liberty of injuring their fellow-creatures, they bless the throne, and the laws upon which it is established.

It is false that the sciences have always been prejudicial to mankind. When they were so, the evil was inevitable. The multiplication of the human species on the face of the earth introduced war, the rudiments of arts, and the first laws, which were temporary compacts arising from necessity, and perishing with it. This was the first philosophy, and its few elements were just, as indolence and want of sagacity, in the early inhabitants of the world, preserved them from error.

But necessities increasing with the number of mankind, stronger and more lasting impressions were necessary to prevent their frequent relapses into a state of barbarity, which became every day more fatal. The first religious errors, which peopled the earth with false divinities, and created a world of invisible beings to govern the visible creation, were of the utmost service to mankind. The greatest benefactors to humanity were those who dared to deceive, and led pliant ignorance to the foot of the altar. By presenting to the minds of the vulgar, things out of the reach of their senses, which fled as they pursued, and always eluded their grasp; which, as they never comprehended, they never despised, their different passions were united, and attached to a single object. This was the first transition of all nations from their savage state. Such was the necessary, and perhaps the only bond of all societies at their first formation. I speak not of the chosen people of God, to whom the most extraordinary miracles, and the most signal favours, supplied the place of human policy. But as it is the nature of error to subdivide itself *ad infinitum,* so the pretended knowledge which sprung from it transformed mankind into a blind fanatic multitude, jarring and destroying each other in the labyrinth in which they were inclosed; hence it is not wonderful, that some sensible and philosophic minds should regret the ancient state of barbarity. This was the first epocha in which knowledge, or rather opinions, were fatal.

The second may be found in the difficult and terrible passage from error to truth, from darkness to light. The violent shock between a mass of errors, useful to the few and powerful, and the truths so important to the many and the weak, with the fermentation of passions excited on that occasion, were productive of infinite evils to unhappy mortals. In the study of history, whose principal periods, after certain intervals, much resemble each other, we frequently find, in the necessary passage from the obscurity of ignorance to the light of philosophy, and from tyranny to liberty, its natural consequence, one generation sacrificed to the happiness of the next. But when this flame is extinguished, and the world delivered from its evils, truth, after a very slow progress, sits down with monarchs on the throne, and is worshiped in the assemblies of nations. Shall we then believe, that light diffused among the people is more destructive than darkness, and that the knowledge of the relations of things can never be fatal to mankind?

Ignorance may indeed be less fatal than a small degree of knowledge, because this adds, to the evils of ignorance, the inevitable errors of a confined view of things on this side the bounds of truth; but a man of enlightened understanding, appointed guardian of the laws, is the greatest blessing that a sovereign can bestow on a nation. Such a man is accustomed to behold truth, and not to fear it; unacquainted with the greatest part of those imaginary and insatiable necessities, which so often put virtue to the proof, and accustomed to contemplate mankind from the most elevated point of view, he considers the nation as his family, and his fellow citizens as brothers; the distance between the great and the vulgar appears to him the less, as the number of mankind he has in view is greater.

The philosopher has necessities and interests unknown to the vulgar, and the chief of these is not to belie in public the principles he taught in obscurity, and the habit of loving virtue for its own sake. A few such philosophers would constitute the happiness of a nation; which however would be but of short duration, unless by good laws the number were so increased as to lessen the probability of an improper choice.

OF MAGISTRATES.

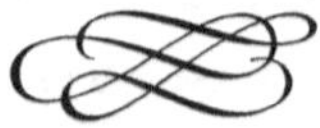

ANOTHER method of preventing crimes is, to make the observance of the laws, and not their violation, the interest of the magistrate.

The greater the number of those who constitute the tribunal, the less is the danger of corruption; because the attempt will be more difficult, and the power and temptation of each individual will be proportionably less. If the sovereign, by pomp and the austerity of edicts, and by refusing to hear the complaints of the oppressed, accustom his subjects to respect the magistrates more than the laws, the magistrates will gain indeed, but it will be at the expence of public and private security.

OF REWARDS.

YET another method of preventing crimes is, to reward virtue. Upon this subject the laws of all nations are silent. If the rewards, proposed by academies for the discovery of useful truths, have increased our knowledge, and multiplied good books, is it not probable that rewards, distributed by the beneficent hand of a sovereign, would also multiply virtuous actions? The coin of honour is inexhaustible, and is abundantly fruitful in the hands of a prince who distributes it wisely.

OF EDUCATION.

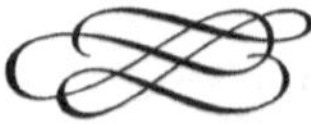

FINALLY, the most certain method of preventing crimes, is to perfect the system of education. But this is an object too vast, and exceeds my plan; an object, if I may venture to declare it, which is so intimately connected with the nature of government, that it will always remain a barren spot, cultivated only by a few wise men.

A great man, who is persecuted by that world he hath enlightened, and to whom we are indebted for many important truths, hath most amply detailed the principal maxims of useful education. This chiefly consists in presenting to the mind a small number of select objects; in substituting the originals for the copies, both of physical and moral phenomena; in leading the pupil to virtue by the easy road of sentiment, and in withholding him from evil by the infallible power of necessary inconveniences, rather than by command, which only obtains counterfeit and momentary obedience.

OF PARDONS.

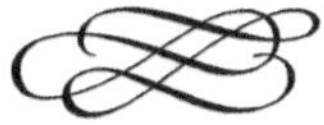

AS punishments become more mild, clemency and pardon are less necessary. Happy the nation in which they will be considered as dangerous! Clemency, which has often been deemed a sufficient substitute for every other virtue in sovereigns, should be excluded in a perfect legislation, where punishments are mild, and the proceedings in criminal cases regular and expeditious. This truth will seem cruel to those who live in countries, where, from the absurdity of the laws, and the severity of punishments, pardons, and the clemency of the prince, are necessary. It is indeed one of the noblest prerogatives of the throne, but, at the same time, a tacit disapprobation of the laws. Clemency is a virtue which belongs to the legislator, and not to the executor of the laws; a virtue which ought to shine in the code, and not in private judgment. To shew mankind, that crimes are sometimes pardoned, and that punishment is not the necessary consequence, is to nourish the flattering hope of impunity, and is the cause of their considering every punishment inflicted as an act of injustice and oppression. The prince, in pardoning, gives up the public security in favour of an individual, and, by his ill-judged benevolence, proclaims a public act of impunity. Let, then, the executors of the laws be inexorable, but let the legislator be tender, indulgent and humane. He is a wise architect, who erects his edifice on the foundation of self-love, and contrives, that the interest of the public shall be the interest of each individual; who is not obliged by particular laws, and irregular proceedings, to separate the public good from that of individuals, and erect the image of public felicity on the basis of fear and distrust; but, like a wise philosopher, he will permit his brethren to enjoy, in quiet, that small portion of happiness, which the immense system, established by the first cause, permits them to taste on this earth, which is but a point in the universe.

A small crime is sometimes pardoned, if the person offended chooses to forgive the offender. This may be an act of good nature and humanity, but it is contrary to the good of the public. The right of punishing belongs not to any individual in particular, but to society in general, or the sovereign. He may renounce his own portion of this right, but cannot give up that of others.

CONCLUSION.

I CONCLUDE with this reflection, that the severity of punishments ought to be in proportion to the state of the nation. Among a people hardly yet emerged from barbarity, they should be most severe, as strong impressions are required; but in proportion as the minds of men become softened by their intercourse in society, the severity of punishments should be diminished, if it be intended, that the necessary relation between the object and the sensation should be maintained.

From what I have written results the following general theorem, of considerable utility, though not conformable to custom, the common legislator of nations.

That a punishment may not be an act of violence, of one or of many, against a private member of society, it should be public, immediate and necessary; the least possible in the case given; proportioned to the crime, and determined by the laws.

A COMMENTARY ON THE BOOK OF CRIMES AND PUNISHMENTS.

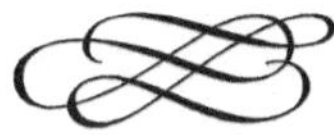

Voltaire

THE OCCASION OF THIS COMMENTARY.

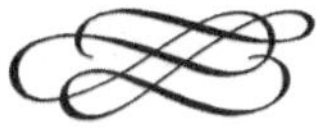

HAVING read, with infinite satisfaction, the little book on Crimes and Punishments, which in morality, as in medicine, may be compared to one of those few remedies, capable of alleviating our sufferings; I flattered myself that it would be a means of softening the remains of barbarism in the laws of many nations; I hoped for some reformation in mankind, when I was informed, that, within a few miles of my abode, they had just hanged a girl of eighteen, beautiful, well made, accomplished, and of a very reputable family.

She was culpable of having suffered herself to be got with child, and also, of having abandoned her infant. This unfortunate girl, flying from her father's house, is taken in labour, and, without assistance, is delivered of her burden by the side of a wood. Shame, which in the sex is a powerful passion, gave her strength to return home, and to conceal her situation. She left her child exposed; it is found the next morning; the mother is discovered, condemned and executed.

The first fault of this unhappy victim ought to have been concealed by the family, or rather claims the protection of the laws, because it was incumbent on her seducer to repair the injury he had done; because weakness hath a right to indulgence; because concealing her pregnancy may endanger her life; because declaring her condition destroys her reputation, and because the difficulty of providing for her infant is a great additional misfortune.

Her second fault is more criminal. She abandons the fruit of her weakness, and exposes it to perish.

But because a child is dead, is it absolutely necessary to kill the mother? She did not kill the child. She flattered herself, that some passenger would have compassion on the innocent babe. It is even possible that she might intend to return and provide for it; a sentiment so natural in the breast of a mother, that it ought to be presumed. The law in the country of which I am speaking is, indeed, positively against her. But is it not an unjust, inhuman, and pernicious law? *Unjust,* because it makes no distinction between her who murders, and her who abandons her infant; *inhuman,* because it punishes with death a too great desire of concealing a weakness; *pernicious,* because it deprives the state of a fruitful subject, in a country that wants inhabitants.

Charity hath not yet established, in that nation, houses of reception for exposed infants. Where charity is wanting, the law is always cruel. It were much better to prevent, than to think only of punishing these frequent misfortunes. The proper object of jurisprudence is, to hinder the commission of crimes, rather than condemn to death a weak woman, when it is evident that her transgression was unattended with malice, and that she hath already been severely punished by the pangs of her own heart.

Insure, as far as possible, a resource to those who shall be tempted to do evil, and you will have less to punish.

OF PUNISHMENTS.

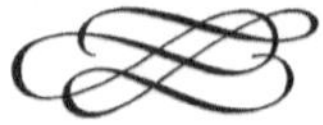

THIS misfortune, and this very hard law, with which I was so sensibly affected, prompted me to cast my eyes on the criminal code of nations. The humane author of the Essay on Crimes and Punishments, had but too much cause to complain, that the latter frequently exceed the former, and are sometimes detrimental to the state they were intended to serve.

Those ingenious punishments, the *ne plus ultra* of the human mind, endeavouring to render death horrible, seem rather the inventions of tyranny than of justice.

The punishment of the *wheel* was first introduced in Germany in the times of anarchy, when those who usurped the regal power resolved to terrify, with unheard-of torments, those who should dispute their authority. In England they ripped open the belly of a man guilty of *high-treason,* tore out his heart, dashed it in his face, and then threw it into the fire. And wherein did this *high-treason* frequently consist? In having been, during a civil war, faithful to an unfortunate king; or, in having spoken freely on the doubtful right of the conqueror. At length, their manners were softened; they continued to tear out the heart, but not till after the death of the offender. The apparatus is dreadful, but the death is mild, if death can ever be mild.

ON THE PUNISHMENT OF HERETICS.

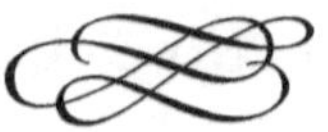

THE denunciation of death to those who, in certain dogmas, differed from the established church, was peculiarly the act of tyranny. No Christian emperor, before the tyrant Maximus, ever thought of condemning a man to punishment merely for points of controversy. It is true, indeed, that two Spanish bishops pursued to death the Priscilianists under Maximus; but it is also true, that this tyrant was willing to gratify the reigning party with the blood of heretics. Barbarity and justice were to him indifferent. Jealous of Theodosius, a Spaniard like himself, he endeavoured to deprive him of the empire of the East, as he had already obtained that of the West. Theodosius was hated for his cruelties; but he had found the means of gaining to his party the heads of the church. Maximus was willing to display the same zeal, and to attach the Spanish bishops to his faction. He flattered both the old and the new religion; he was as treacherous as inhuman, as indeed were all those who at that time either pretended to, or obtained empire. That vast part of the world was then governed like Algiers at present. Emperors were created and dethroned by the military power, and were often chosen from among nations that were reputed barbarous. Theodosius opposed to his competitor other barbarians from Scythia. He filled the army with Goths, and surprised Alaric the conqueror of Rome. In this horrible confusion, each endeavoured to strengthen his party by every means in his power.

Maximus having caused the Emperor Gratian, the colleague of Theodosius, to be assassinated at Lyons, meditated the destruction of Valentinian the second, who, during his infancy, had been made successor to Gratian. He assembled at Treves a powerful army, composed of Gauls and Germans. He caused troops to be levied in Spain, when two Spanish bishops, Idacio and Ithacus, or Itacius, both men of credit, came and demanded of him the blood of Priscilian, and all his adherents, who were of opinion, that souls were emanations from God; that the Trinity did not contain three hypostases; and moreover, they carried their sacrilege so far as to fast on Sundays. Maximus, half Pagan, and half Christian, soon perceived the enormity of these crimes. The holy bishops, Idacio and Itacius, obtained leave to torture Priscilian and his accomplices before they were put to death. They were both present, that things might be done according to order, and they returned blessing God, and numbering Maximus, the defender of the faith, among the saints. But Maximus being afterward defeated by Theodosius, and assassinated at the feet of his conqueror, had not the good fortune to be canonized.

It is proper to observe, that Saint Martin, bishop of Tours, who was really a good man, solicited the pardon of Priscilian; but being himself accused of heresy by the bishops, he returned to Tours, for fear of the torture at Treves.

As to Priscilian, he had the consolation, after he was hanged, of being honoured by his sect as a martyr. His feast was celebrated, and would be celebrated still, if there were any Priscilianists remaining.

This example made the entire church tremble; but it was soon after imitated and surpassed. Priscilianists had been put to death by the sword, the halter, and by lapidation. A young lady of quality, suspected to have fasted on a Sunday, was at Bourdeaux *only* stoned to death. These punishments appeared too mild; it was proved that God required that heretics should be roasted alive. The peremptory argument, in support of this opinion was, that God punishes them in that manner in the next world, and that every prince, or his representative, even down to a petty constable, is the image of God in this sublunary world.

On this principle it was, that all over Europe they burnt witches and sorcerers, who were manifestly under the empire of the devil; and also heterodox Christians, which were deemed still more criminal and dangerous.

It is not certainly known, what was the crime of

those priests who were burnt at Orleans in the presence of king Robert and his wife Constantia, in the year 1022. How indeed should it be known? there being, at that time, but a small number of clerks and monks that could write. All we certainly know is, that Robert and his wife feasted their eyes with this abominable spectacle. One of the sectaries had been confessor to her majesty, who thought she could not better repair the misfortune of having confessed to a heretic, than by seeing him devoured by the flames.

Custom becomes law; from that period to the present time, a space of more than seven hundred years, the church hath continued to burn those that are guilty, or supposed guilty, of an error in opinion.

ON THE EXTIRPATION OF HERESY.

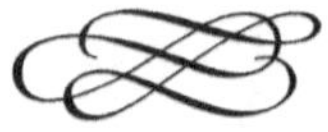

IT seems necessary to distinguish an heresy of opinion from faction. From the first ages of Christianity opinions have been different. The Christians of Alexandria were, in many points, of a different opinion from those of Antioch. The Achaians differed from the Asiatics. This diversity of opinion existed from the beginning, and probably will continue for ever. Jesus Christ, who could have united all the faithful in the same sentiments, did it not; and therefore we may conclude that it was not his design; but that he chose rather to exercise all his churches in acts of indulgence and charity, by permitting different systems, yet all agreeing to acknowledge him their lord and master. These several sects, so long as they were tolerated by the emperors, or concealed from their sight, had it not in their power to prosecute each other, being equally subject to the Roman magistrates; they could only dispute. If they were persecuted, they equally claimed the privilege of nature: "Suffer us," they said, "to adore our God in peace, and do not refuse us the liberty you grant to the Jews:" Every sect may now urge the same argument to their oppressors. They may say to those who want privileges to the Jews; "Treat us as you treat the sons of Jacob; let us, like them, pray to God according to our conscience. Our opinion will no more injure your state, than Judaism. You tolerate the enemies of Jesus Christ, tolerate us who adore him, and who differ from you only in theological subtleties. Do not deprive yourselves of useful subjects; useful in your manufactures, your marine, and the cultivation of your lands. Of what importance is it, that their creed be somewhat different from yours? You want their labour, and not their catechism?"

Faction is quite a different thing. It always happens, that a persecuted sect degenerates into faction. The oppressed naturally unite and animate each other; and are generally more industrious in strengthening their party, than their persecutors in their extermination. They must either destroy or be destroyed. So it happened after the persecution excited in 304, by Galerius, in the two last years of Dioclesian. The Christians, having been favoured by that emperor during eighteen years, were become too numerous and too rich to be exterminated. They joined Chlorus; they fought for his son Constantine, and a total revolution of the empire was the consequence.

Small events may be compared with great, when they are produced by the same spirit. Revolutions of a similar kind happened in Holland, in Scotland,

and in Switzerland. When Ferdinand and Isabella
drove the Jews out of Spain, where they were established not only before the reigning family, but before the Moors, the Goths, or even the
Carthaginians; if the Jews had been as warlike as
they were rich, they might easily, in conjunction
with the Arabs, have effected a revolution.

In short, no sect ever changed the government,
unless excited by despair. Mahomed himself succeeded only because he was driven from Mecca,
and a reward offered for his head.

Would you prevent a sect from overturning the
state, imitate the present wise conduct of England,
of Germany, of Holland; use toleration. The only
methods, in policy, to be taken with a new sect, are,
to put to death the chief and all his adherents, men,
women, and children, without sparing one individual; or to tolerate them, when numerous. The first
method is that of a monster; the second of a
wise man.

Chain your subjects to the state by their interest.
Let the Quaker and the Turk find their advantage in
living under your laws. Religion is of God to man;
the civil law is of you to your people.

OF PROFANATION.

LEWIS IX. king of France, who for his virtues was numbered among the saints, made a law against blasphemers. He condemned them to a new punishment; their tongues were pierced with a hot iron. It was a kind of retaliation; the sinning member suffering the punishment. But it was somewhat difficult to determine what was blasphemy. Expressions frequently escape from a man in a passion, from joy, or even in conversation, which are merely expletives, such as the *sela* and the *vab* of the Hebrews, the *pol* and the *ædepol* of the Latins, as also *per Deos immortales,* an expression frequently used, without the least intention of swearing by the immortal gods.

The words which are called oaths and blasphemy, are commonly vague terms that may be variously interpreted. The law by which they are punished, seems to be founded on that of the Jews, which says: *Thou shalt not take the name of the Lord thy God in vain.* The best commentators are of opinion, that this commandment relates to perjury; and there is the more reason to believe them right, as the word *shave,* which is translated *in vain,* properly signifies perjury. Now, what analogy can there be between perjury and *Cabo de Dios, Cadedis, Sangbleu, Ventrebleu, Corpo de Dio,* etc.?

It was customary with the Jews to swear by the life of God, *as the Lord liveth:* the phrase was common; so that it was lying in the name of God that was forbidden.

Philip Augustus, in 1181, condemned the nobility who should pronounce the words which are softened in the terms *Tetebleu, Ventrebleu, Corbleu, Sangbleu,* to pay a fine, and the plebeians to be drowned. The first part of this law seems puerile, the latter abominable. It was an outrage to nature, to drown one man for a crime for which another paid a few pence of the money of those times. So that this law, like many other, remained unexecuted, especially when the king was excommunicated, and his kingdom interdicted by Pope Celestine III.

Saint Lewis, transported with zeal, ordered indiscriminately, that whosoever should pronounce these indecent words, should have his tongue bored, or his upper lip cut off. A citizen of Paris, having suffered this punishment, complained to Pope Innocent IV. This pontiff remonstrated to the king that the punishment was too great for the crime, which however had no effect upon his majesty. Happy had it been for mankind, if the popes had never affected any other superiority over kings.

The ordinance of Lewis XIV. says, "Those who shall be convicted of having sworn by, or blasphemed the holy name of God, of his most holy mother, or of his saints, shall, for the first offence, pay a fine; for the second, third, and fourth, a double, triple, and quadruple fine; for the fifth, shall be put in the stocks; for the sixth, shall stand in the pillory, and lose his upper lip; for the seventh, shall have his tongue cut out."

This law appears to be humane and just, as it inflicts a cruel punishment only on a seven-fold repetition, which can hardly be presumed.

But with regard to more atrocious profanations, which are called Sacrilege, the criminal ordinance mentions only robbing of churches; it takes no notice of public impieties, perhaps because they were not supposed to happen, or were too difficult to specify. They are left therefore to the discretion of the judge; and yet nothing ought to be left to discretion.

In such extraordinary cases, how is the judge to act? He should consider the age of the offender, the nature and degree of his offence, and particularly the necessity of a public example. *Pro qualitate personæ, quoque rei conditione et temporis et ætatis et sexus, vel clementius statuendum.* If the law does not expressly say that such a crime shall be punished with death, what judge shall think himself authorised to pronounce that sentence? If the law be silent; if nevertheless a punishment be required, the judge ought certainly, without hesitation, to decree the least severe, because he is a man.

Sacrilegious profanations are never committed

except by young debauchees. Would you punish them as severely as if they had murdered a brother? Their youth pleads in their favour. They are not suffered to dispose of their possessions, because they are supposed to want maturity of judgment, sufficient to foresee the consequences of an imprudent transaction. Is it not therefore natural to suppose, that they are incapable of foreseeing the consequences of their impiety?

Would you treat a wild young man, who, in his phrenzy, had profaned a sacred image, without stealing it, with the same rigour that you punished a Brinvilliers, who poisoned his father and his whole family?

There is no law against the unhappy youth, and you are determined to make one that shall condemn him to the severest punishment! He deserved chastisement, but did he deserve such excruciating torture, and the most horrible death?

But he had offended God! True, most grievously. Imitate God in your proceedings against him. If he be penitent, God forgives him. Impose a penance, and let him be pardoned.

Your illustrious *Montesquieu* hath said: It is our duty to honour the Deity, and not to revenge him. Let us weigh these words. They do not mean, that we should neglect the maintenance of public decorum; but, as the judicious author of the preceding Essay observes, that it is absurd for an insect to pretend to revenge the Supreme Being. A village magistrate, or the magistrate of a city, is neither a Moses nor a Joshua.

OF THE INDULGENCE OF THE ROMANS IN MATTERS OF RELIGION.

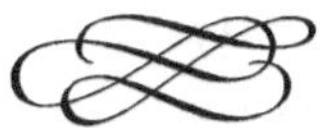

THE amazing contrast between the Roman laws, and the barbarous institutions by which they were succeeded, hath often been the subject of conversation among the speculative part of mankind.

Doubtless the Roman senate held the supreme God in as great veneration as we; and professed as much esteem for their secondary deities as we for our saints. *Ab Jove principium* was their common formule. Pliny, in his panegyric on the good Trajan, attests, that the Romans never omitted to begin their discourse and affairs by invoking the Deity. Cicero and Livy tell us the same thing. No people were more religious; but they were too wise, and too great, to descend to the punishment of idle language or philosophic opinions. They were incapable of inflicting barbarous punishments on those who, with Cicero, himself an augur, had no faith in auguries; or on those who, like Cæsar, asserted in full senate, that the gods do not punish men after death.

It hath often been remarked that the senate permitted the chorus in the Troad to sing, There is nothing after death, and death itself is nothing. You ask, what becomes of the dead? They are where they were ere they were born.[1]

Was ever profanation more flagrant than this? From Ennius to Ausonius all his profanation, notwithstanding the respect for divine worship. Why were these things disregarded by the senate? Because they did not, in any wise, affect the government of the state; because they disturbed no institution, nor religious ceremony. The *police* of the Romans was nevertheless excellent; they were nevertheless absolute masters of the best part of the world, till the reign of Theodosius the second.

It was a maxim of the Romans, *Deorum offensæ, Diis curæ,* Offences against the gods concern the gods only. The senate, by the wisest institution, being at the head of religion, were under no apprehensions that a convocation of priests should force them to revenge the priesthood under a pretext of revenging Heaven. They never said, let us tear the impious asunder, lest we ourselves be deemed impious; let us shew the priesthood, by our cruelty, that we are no less religious than they.

But our religion is more holy than that of the Romans, and consequently impiety is a greater crime. Granted. God will punish it. The part of man is, to punish that which is criminal in the public disorder which the impiety hath occasioned. But if in the act of impiety the delinquent hath not even stolen a handkerchief; if the ceremonies of religion have been in no wise disturbed, shall we, as I said before, punish the impiety as we would punish parricide? The Marshal d'Ancre had caused a white cock to be killed when the moon was at full: ought we therefore to burn the Marshal D'Ancre?

Est modus in rebus, sunt certi denique fines;
Nec scutica dignum horribili sectere flagello.

---

1. *Post mortem nihil est, mors ipsaque nihil, etc. SENECA.*

ON THE CRIME OF
PREACHING; AND OF
ANTHONY.

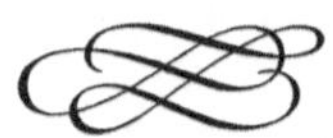

ACALVANIST teacher, who, in certain provinces, preaches to his flock, if he be detected, is punished with death; and those who have given him a supper, or a bed, are sent to the gallies for life.

In other countries, if a Jesuit be caught preaching, he is hanged. Is it to avenge God that this Calvinist and this Jesuit are put to death? Have both parties built upon the following Evangelical law? *If he neglect to hear the church, let him be unto thee as an heathen man and a publican.* But the Evangelist does not order that this heathen and this publican should be hanged.

Or have they built on this passage in Deuteronomy: [1] *If among you a prophet arise; and that which he hath said come to pass; and he sayeth unto you, let us follow strange gods; and if thy brother, or thy son, or thy wife, or the friend of thy heart, say unto thee, Come, let us*

The counsellor Dubourg, the monk Jehan Chouvin, named Calvin, the Spanish physician Servetus, the Calabrian Gentilis, all worshipped the same God: and yet the president Minard caused counsellor Dubourg to be burnt; and Dubourg's friends caused president Minard to be assassinated; Jehan Calvin caused the physician Servetus to be roasted; and had likewise the consolation to be a principal means of bringing the Calabrian Gentilis to the block; and the successors of Jehan Calvin burnt Anthony. Was it reason, or piety, or justice, that committed these murders?

This history of Anthony is one of the most singular which the annals of phrenzy hath preserved. I read the following account in a very curious manuscript; it is in part related by Jacob Spon.

Anthony was born at Brieu in Lorrain, of catholic parents, and he was educated by the Jesuits at Pont a Mousson. The preacher Feri engaged him in the protestant religion at Metz. Having returned to Nancy he was prosecuted as a heretic, and, had he not been saved by a friend, would certainly have been hanged. He fled for refuge to Sedan, where, being taken for a Papist, he narrowly escaped assassination.

Seeing by what strange fatality his life was not in safety, either among Papists or Protestants, he went to Venice and turned Jew. He was positively

persuaded, even to the last moments of his life, that
the religion of the Jews was the only true religion;
for that, if it was once true, it must always be so.
The Jews did not circumcise him, for fear of offending the state; but he was no less internally a
Jew. He now went to Geneva, where, concealing his
faith, he became a preacher, was president of the
college, and finally what is called a minister.

The perpetual combat in his breast between the
religion of Calvin, which he was obliged to preach,
and that of Moses, which was the only religion he
believed, produced a long illness. He became
melancholy, and at last quite mad, crying aloud,
that he was a Jew. The ministers of the gospel came
to visit him, and endeavoured to bring him to himself; but he answered, "that he adored none but the
God of Israel; that it was impossible for God to
change; that God could never have given a law, and
inscribed it with his own hand, with an intention
that it should be abolished." He spoke against
Christianity, and afterwards retracted all he had
said, and even wrote his confession of faith, to escape punishment; but the unhappy persuasion of
his heart would not permit him to sign it. The
council of the city assembled the clergy, to consult
what was to be done with the unfortunate Anthony.
The minority of these clergy were of opinion, that
they should have compassion on him, and rather
endeavour to cure his disease than punish him. The
majority determined that he should be burnt, and
he was burnt. This transaction is of the year 1632. [2]
A hundred years of reason and virtue are scarce sufficient to expiate such a deed.

1. Chap. xiii.
2. Spon, p. 500. Guy Vances.

THE HISTORY OF SIMON MORIN.

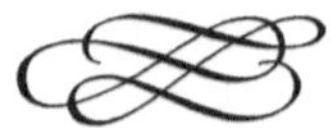

THE tragical end of Simon Morin is not less horrible than that of poor Anthony. It was midst the feasting, pleasures, and gallantry of a brilliant court; it was even in the times of the greatest licentiousness, that this unfortunate madman was burnt at Paris, in the year 1663. Imagining that he had seen visions, he carried his folly so far, as to believe that he was sent from God, and that he was incorporated with Jesus Christ.

The Parliament very wisely condemned him to be confined in a mad-house. What was very remarkable, there happened to be confined in the same mad-house another fool, who called himself God the Father. Simon Morin was so struck with the folly of his companion, that he acknowledged his own, and appeared for a time to have recovered his senses. He declared his repentance, and, unfortunately for himself, obtained his liberty.

Some time after, he relapsed into his former nonsense, and began to dogmatize. His unhappy destiny brought him acquainted with St. Sorlin Desmarets, who, for some months, was his friend, but who afterwards, from jealousy, became his most cruel persecutor.

This Desmarets was no less a visionary than Morin. His first follies indeed were innocent. He printed the Tragi-Comedies of *Erigone* and *Mirame,* with a translation of the Psalms; the Romance of Ariane, and the Poem of Clovis, with the office of the holy Virgin turned into verse. He likewise published dithyrambic poems, enriched with invectives against Homer and Virgil. From this kind of follies he proceeded to others of a more serious nature. He attacked *Port-Royal,* and after confessing that he had perverted some women to atheism, he commenced prophet. He pretended that God had given him, with his own hand, the key to the treasure of the Apocalypse, that with this key he would reform the whole world, and that he should command an army of an hundred and forty thousand men against the Jansenists.

Nothing could have been more reasonable and more just, than to have confined him in the same place with Simon Morin; but can it be believed, that he found credit with the Jesuit Annat, the king's confessor? whom he persuaded, that this poor Simon Morin would establish a sect almost as dangerous as the Jansenists themselves. In short, carrying his infamy so far as to turn informer, he obtained an order to seize the person of his rival. Shall I tell it! Simon Morin was condemned to be burnt alive?

In conducting him to the stake, there was found, in one of his stockings, a paper in which he begged forgiveness of God for all his errors. This ought to have saved him; but no: the sentence was confirmed, and he was executed without mercy.

Such deeds are enough to make a man's hair bristle with horror. Yet where is the country that hath not beheld such shocking spectacles? Mankind universally forget that they are brothers, and persecute each other even to death. Let us console ourselves with the hope, that such dreadful times are passed, never more to return.

OF WITCHES.

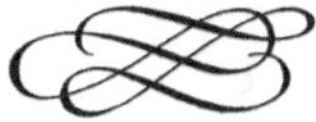

IN the year 1748, in the bishopric of Wurtsburg, an old woman was convicted of witchcraft and burnt. This was an extraordinary phenomenon in the present century. But how incredible it seems, that a people, who boasted of their reformation, and of having trampled superstition under their feet, and who flattered themselves that they had brought their reason to perfection; is it not wonderful, I say, that such a people should have believed in witchcraft; should have burnt old women accused of this crime, and that above a hundred years after the pretended reformation of their reason?

In the year 1652, a country woman, named Michelle Chaudron, of the little territory of Geneva, met the devil in her way from the city. The devil gave her a kiss, received her homage, and imprinted on her upper lip and on her right breast, the mark which he is wont to bestow upon his favourites. This seal of the devil is a little sign upon the skin, which renders it insensible, as we are assured by all the demonographical civilians of those times.

The devil ordered Michelle Chaudron to bewitch two young girls. She obeyed her master punctually. The parents of the two girls accused her of dealing with the devil. The girls, being confronted with the criminal, declared, that they felt a continual prickling in some parts of their bodies, and that they were possessed. Physicians were called, at least men that passed for physicians in those days. They visited the girls. They sought for the seal of the devil on the body of Michelle, which seal is called, in the verbal process, the *Satanical mark*. Into one of these marks they plunged a long needle, which was already no small torture. Blood issued from the wound, and Michelle testified by her cries that the part was not insensible. The judges not finding sufficient proof that Michelle Chaudron was a witch, ordered her to be tortured, which infallibly produced the proof they wanted. The poor wretch, overcome by torment, confessed at last every thing they desired.

The physicians sought again for the Satanical mark, and found it in a little black spot on one of her thighs. Into this they plunged their needle. The poor creature, exhausted and almost expiring with the pain of the torture, was insensible to the needle, and did not cry out. She was instantly condemned to be burnt; but the world beginning at this time to be a little more civilized, she was previously strangled.

At this period every tribunal in Europe resounded with such judgments, and fire and faggot were universally employed against witchcraft as well as heresy. The Turks were reproached with having amongst them neither sorcerers, witches, nor demoniacs; and the want of the latter was considered as an infallible proof of the falsity of their religion.

A zealous friend to the public welfare, to humanity, and to true religion, in one of his writings in favour of innocence, informs us, that there have been above a hundred thousand witches condemned to die by Christian tribunals. If, to these lawful massacres, we add the much superior number of heretics sacrificed, our part of the globe will appear one vast scaffold covered with executioners and victims, and surrounded by judges, guards, and spectators.

ON THE PUNISHMENT OF DEATH.

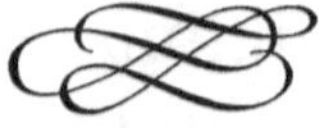

IT hath long since been observed, that a man
after he is hanged is good for nothing, and that
punishments invented for the good of society,
ought to be useful to society. It is evident, that a
score of stout robbers, condemned for life to some
public work, would serve the state in their punishment, and that hanging them is a benefit to nobody
but the executioner. Thieves, in England, are seldom
punished with death, but are transported to the
colonies. This is also practised in Russia, where not
one criminal was executed during the whole reign
of the autocratical Elisabeth. Catherine II. who hath
succeeded her, with much more genius, follows her
example; yet crimes are not multiplied by this humanity; and it generally happens that the criminals
sent to Siberia in time become honest people. The
same is observed in the English colonies. We are astonished at the change, and yet nothing can be more

natural. The condemned are forced to continual labour for a livelihood. The opportunities of vice are wanting. They marry and multiply. Oblige men to work, and you certainly make them honest. It is well known, that atrocious crimes are not committed in the country, unless when there is too much holiday, and consequently too much idleness, and consequently too much debauchery.

The Romans never condemned a citizen to death, unless for crimes which concerned the safety of the state. These our masters, our first legislators, were careful of the blood of their fellow-citizens; but we are extravagant with the blood of ours.

The question hath been frequently debated, whether a judge ought to have the power to punish with death, when the punishment is undetermined by the law? This question was solemnly agitated in the presence of the Emperor Henry VII. who decreed that no judge should have such a power.[1]

There are some criminal cases which are either so new, so complicated, and so unaccountable as to have escaped the provision of the laws, and which, therefore, in some countries are left to the discretion of the judge. But for one case in which the laws permit the death of a criminal whom they have not condemned, there are a thousand wherein humanity should save whom the laws have condemned to suffer.

The sword of justice is in our hands, but we ought rather to blunt than to sharpen its edge. It remains within its sheath in the presence of kings, to inform us that it ought seldom to be drawn.

There have been some judges who were passionately fond of spilling human blood; such was Jef-
feries in England, and such in France was the man
whom they called *Coupe-tete*. Nature never intended
such men for magistrates, but for executioners.

---

1. Boudin de Republica, lib. iii, c. 5.

ON DEATH WARRANTS.

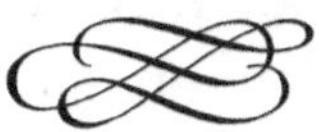

MUST we go to the end of the world, must we have recourse to the laws of China, to learn how frugal we ought to be of human blood? It is now more than four thousand years that the tribunals of that empire have existed; and it is also more than four thousand years that the meanest subject, at the extremity of the empire, hath not been executed without first transmitting his case to the emperor, who causes it to be thrice examined by one of his tribunals; after which he signs the death warrant, alters the sentence, or entirely acquits.

But it is unnecessary to travel so far for examples of this nature; Europe will abundantly supply us. In England, no criminal is put to death, whose death warrant is not signed by the king. It is also practised in Germany, and in most parts of the north. Such likewise was formerly the custom in France, and such it ought to be in all polished nations. A sentence, at a distance from the throne, may be dictated by cabal, prejudice, or ignorance. Such little intrigues are unknown to monarchs, who are continually surrounded by great objects. The members of the supreme council are more enlightened, less liable to prejudice, and better qualified than a provincial judge, to determine whether the state require severe punishments. In short, when inferior courts have judged according to the letter of the law, which possibly may be rigorous, the council mitigates the sentence according to the true spirit of all laws, which teaches, never to sacrifice a man, but in evident necessity.

ON TORTURE.

ALL mankind being exposed to the attempts of violence or perfidy, detest the crimes of which they may possibly be the victims: all desire that the principal offender and his accomplices may be punished; nevertheless, there is a natural compassion in the human heart, which makes all men detest the cruelty of torturing the accused in order to extort confession. The law has not condemned them, and yet, though uncertain of their crime, you inflict a punishment more horrible than that which they are to suffer when their guilt is confirmed. "Possibly thou mayst be innocent; but I will torture thee that I may be satisfied: not that I intend to make thee any recompence for the thousand deaths which I have made thee suffer, in lieu of that which is preparing for thee." Who does not shudder at the idea? St. Augustin opposed such cruelty. The Romans tortured their slaves only; and Quintilian, recollecting that they were men, reproved the Romans for such want of humanity.

If there were but one nation in the world which had abolished the use of torture; if in that nation crimes were no more frequent than in others; and if that nation be more enlightened and more flourishing since the abolition, its example surely were sufficient for the rest of the world. England alone might instruct all other nations in this particular; but England is not the only nation. Torture hath been abolished in other countries, and with success; the question therefore is decided. Shall not a people, who pique themselves on their politeness, pride themselves also on their humanity? Shall they obstinately persist in their inhumanity, merely because it is an ancient custom? Reserve, at least, such cruelty for the punishment of those hardened wretches, who shall have assassinated the father of a family, or the father of his country; but that a young person, who commits a fault which leaves no traces behind it, should suffer equally with a parricide; is not this an useless piece of barbarity?

I am ashamed of having said any thing on this subject, after what hath been already said by the author of the Essay on Crimes and Punishments. I ought to have been satisfied with wishing, that mankind may read with attention the work of that friend to humanity.

OF CERTAIN SANGUINARY TRIBUNALS.

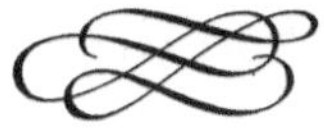

IS it credible, that there formerly existed a supreme tribunal more horrible than the Inquisition, and that this tribunal was established by Charlemagne? It was the judgment of Westphalia, otherwise called the Vhemic Court. The severity, or rather cruelty, of this court, went so far as to punish with death, every Saxon who broke his fast during Lent. The same law was also established in *Franche-Comte,* in the beginning of the seventeenth century. In the archives of a little place called St. Claude, situated in a remote corner of the most mountainous part of the county of Burgundy, are preserved the particulars of the sentence and verbal process of execution of a poor gentleman named Claude Guillon, who was beheaded on the 28th of July, 1629. Being reduced to the utmost poverty, and urged by the most intolerable hunger, he eat, on a fish-day, a morsel of horse flesh, which had been killed in a neighbouring field. This was his crime. He was found guilty of sacrilege. Had he been a rich man, and had spent two hundred crowns in a supper of sea-fish, suffering the poor to die of hunger, he would have been considered as a person fulfilling every duty. The following is a copy of his sentence: "Having seen all the papers of the process, and heard the opinions of the doctors learned in the law, we declare the said Claude Guillon to be truly attainted and convicted of having taken away part of the flesh of a horse, killed in the meadow of that town; of having caused the said flesh to be dressed, and of eating the same on Saturday the 31st of March," etc.

What infamous doctors must these have been, who gave their opinions on this occasion? Was it among the Topinambous, or among the Hottentots, that these things happened? The Vhemic Court was yet more horrible. Delegates from this court were secretly spread over all Germany, taking informations unknown to the accused, who were condemned without being heard; and frequently, in want of an executioner, the youngest judge performed the office himself. [1] It was requisite, in order to be safe from the assassination of this court, to procure letters of exemption from the emperor; and even these were sometimes ineffectual. This chamber of assassins was not entirely abolished till the reign of Maximilian I. It ought to have been dissolved in the blood of its members. The Venetian Council of Ten was, in comparison with this, a court of mercy.

What shall we think of such horrid proceedings? Is it sufficient to bewail humanity? There were some cases that cried aloud for vengeance.

------

1. See the excellent abridgement of the chronological history and laws of Germany, an. 803.

ON THE DIFFERENCE BETWEEN POLITICAL AND NATURAL LAWS.

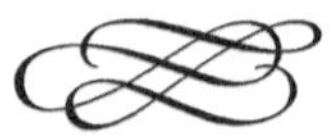

I CALL *natural* laws, those which nature dictates in all ages to all men, for the maintenance of that justice which she (say what they will of her) hath implanted in our hearts. Theft, violence, homicide, ingratitude to beneficent parents, perjury against innocence, conspiracies against one's country, are crimes that are universally and justly punished, though with more or less severity.

I call *political* laws, those that are made in compliance with present necessity, whether it be to give stability to the government, or to prevent misfortune. For example; being apprehensive that the enemy may receive intelligence from the inhabitants of the city, you shut the gates, and forbid any one to pass the ramparts on pain of death.

Or, fearful of a new sect of people, who publicly disclaim all obedience to their sovereign, and secretly consult of means to divest themselves of that obedience; who preach, that all men are equal, and that obedience is due to God alone; who, accusing the reigning sect of superstition, mean to destroy that which is consecrated by the state; you denounce death against those who, in publicly dogmatizing in favour of this sect, may instigate the people to revolt.

Or, two ambitious princes contend for a crown: the strongest gains the prize, and punishes with death the partizans of the weaker. The judges become the instruments of vengeance of the new sovereign, and the supports of his authority.

When Richard the Third, the murderer of his two nephews, was acknowledged king of England, the jury found Sir William Collinburn guilty of having written to a friend of the Duke of Richmond, who was at that time raising an army, and who afterwards reigned by the name of Henry VII. They found two ridiculous lines of Sir William's writing, which were sufficient to condemn him to a horrible death. History abounds with such examples of justice.

The right of reprisal is also a law adopted by nations. For example, your enemy has hanged one of your brave captains, for having defended an old ruined castle against a whole army. One of *his* captains falls into your hands; he is a worthy man, and you esteem him; nevertheless you hang him by way of reprisal. You say it is the law: that is to say, because your enemy has been guilty of an enormous crime, you must be guilty of another.

These political sanguinary laws exist but for a

time; they are temporary, because they are not founded in truth. They resemble the necessity which, in cases of extreme famine, obliges people to eat each other: they cease to eat men as soon as bread is to be had.

ON THE CRIME OF HIGH-TREASON. ON TITUS OATES, AND ON THE DEATH OF AUGUSTIN DE THOU.

HIGH-TREASON is an offence committed against the security of the commonwealth, or of the king its representative. It is considered as parricide, and therefore ought not to be extended to offences which bear no analogy to that crime. In making it high-treason to commit a theft in any house belonging to the state, or even to speak seditious words, you lessen the horror which the crime of high-treason ought to inspire.

In our ideas of great crimes, there should be nothing arbitrary. If a theft from, or imprecation against, a father be considered as parricide, you break the bond of filial piety; the son will then regard his parent as a terrible monster. Every exaggeration in a law tends to its destruction.

In common crimes, the laws of England are favourable to the accused; but in cases of high-treason they are against him. The Jesuit Titus Oates being legally interrogated in the House of Commons, and having upon his oath declared, that he had related the *whole* truth, yet afterwards accused the secretary of the Duke of York, and several others, of high-treason, and his information was admitted. He likewise swore before the king's council, that he had not seen the secretary, and afterwards that he had. Notwithstanding these illegalities and contradictions, the secretary was executed.

The same Titus Oates and another witness deposed, that fifty Jesuits had conspired to assassinate Charles II. and that they had seen commissions, signed by father Oliva, general of the Jesuits, for the officers that were to command an army of rebels. This evidence was sufficient to authorize the tearing out the hearts of several people, and dashing them in their faces. But seriously, can two witnesses be thought sufficient to convict a man whom they have a mind to destroy? At least one would imagine they ought not to be notorious villains; neither ought that which they depose to be improbable.

Let us suppose that two of the most upright magistrates in the kingdom were to accuse a man of having conspired with the Mufti, to circumcise the whole Council of State, the Parliament, the Archbishop and the Sorbonne; in vain these two magistrates might swear, that they had seen the letters of the Mufti: it would naturally be supposed that they were wrong in their heads. It was equally ridiculous to imagine, that the general of the Jesuits should raise an army in England, as that the Mufti intended to circumcise the Court of France. But unhappily

Titus Oates was believed; that there might remain no species of atrocious folly, which hath not entered into the heart of man.

The laws of England do not consider as guilty of conspiracy those who are privy to it, and do not inform. They suppose the informer as infamous as the conspirator is culpable. In France, if any one be privy to a conspiracy, and does not reveal it, he is punished with death. Lewis XI. against whom conspiracies were frequent, made this law; a law which a Lewis XII. or a Henry IV. could never have imagined. It not only obliges an honest man to divulge a crime, which, by his resolution and advice, he might possibly prevent; but it renders him liable to be punished as a calumniator, it being easy for the accused to manage their affairs in such a manner as to elude conviction.

This was exactly the case of the truly respectable Augustin de Thou, counsellor of state, and son of the only good historian of which France can boast; equal to Guicciardini in point of abilities, and perhaps superior in point of impartiality.

This conspiracy was against Cardinal de Richelieu, rather than against Lewis XIII. The design was not to betray France to an enemy; for the king's brother, who was the principal author of the plot, could never intend to betray a kingdom to which he was the presumptive heir, there being only between him and the crown a dying brother, and two children in the cradle.

De Thou was neither guilty in the sight of God nor man. One of the agents of the king's brother, of the Duke of Bouillon, sovereign prince of Sedan, and of the grand Equerry d'Effiat St. Mars, had communicated their intention to de Thou, who immediately went to St. Mars, and endeavoured to dissuade him from the enterprize. If he had informed against him, he had no proof, and must inevitably have fallen a sacrifice to the resentment of the presumptive heir of a sovereign prince, of the king's favourite, and to public execration. In short, he would have been punished as a malignant calumniator.

The chancellor Seguier was convinced of this in confronting de Thou with the grand Equerry, when de Thou asked the latter the following question: "Do you not remember, Sir, that there never passed a day, in which I did not endeavour to dissuade you from the attempt?" St. Mars acknowledged it to be true. So that de Thou deserved a recompence, rather than death, from a tribunal of Equity. He certainly deserved to have been saved by Cardinal Richelieu; but humanity was not his virtue. There is in this case something more than *summum jus summa injuria.* In the sentence of this worthy man we read, "for having had knowledge and participation of the said conspiracy." It does not say for not having revealed. So that his crime was, his having been informed of a crime; and he was punished for having had ears and eyes.

All that we can say in extenuation of the severity is, that it was not the act of Justice herself, but of a delegated power. The *letter* of the law was positive; but I appeal not only to the lawyers, but to all

mankind, whether the *spirit* of the law was not perverted? It is a melancholy absurdity, that a small
number of people should condemn as criminal, a
man judged innocent by a whole nation, and worth
their esteem!

OF RELIGIOUS CONFESSION.

JAURIGNY and Balthazar Gerard, who assassinated William I. Prince of Orange; Clement the Dominican, Chatel, Ravaillac, and all the other parricides of those times, went to confession before they committed their crimes. Fanaticism, in that deplorable age, was carried to such excess, that confession was an additional engagement to the perpetration of villainy; an engagement deemed sacred, because confession is a sacrament.

Strada himself says, that Jaurigny non ante facinus aggredi sustinuit quam expiatam necis animam apud Dominicanum sacerdotem cælesti pane firmaverit.

It appears in the interrogatory of Ravaillac that coming from the *Feuillants,* and going towards the Jesuits college, he addressed himself to the Jesuit d'Aubigny; that after talking to him of several apparitions which he had seen, he shewed him a knife, on the blade of which was engraved a heart and a cross; and that he said, *this heart signifies, that the heart of the king should be induced to make war against the Huguenots.* If this d'Aubigny had informed the king of these words, and described the man, the best of kings might possibly have escaped assassination.

On the 20th of August, 1610, three months after the death of Henry IV. whose wounds were yet bleeding in the hearts of his subjects, the advocate-general Servin, of illustrious memory, required that the Jesuits should be obliged to sign the four following articles:

I. That the Council is superior to the Pope.

II. That the Pope cannot deprive the king of any of his rights by excommunication.

III. That the ecclesiastics are, like other people, entirely subject to the king.

IV. That a priest who, by confession, is apprized of a conspiracy against the king or the state, should reveal it to the magistrates.

On the 22d, the parliament published an *arret,* forbidding the Jesuits to instruct youth, until they had signed those four articles. But the court of Rome was at that time so powerful, and that of France so weak, that the *arret* was disregarded.

It is worth notice, that this court of Rome, which would not suffer confession to be revealed when the life of a sovereign was concerned, obliged the confessors to inform the Inquisition in case any female should accuse another priest of having seduced or attempted to seduce her. Paul IV. Pius IV. Clement VIII. and Gregory XV. ordered this revelation. It was a dangerous snare both for the confessor and the penitent. It was converting a sacrament into a register of accusations and sacrilege; for by the ancient canons, and particularly by the Lateran council, under Innocent III. every confessor who reveals confession, of whatsoever nature it may be, shall be interdicted and imprisoned for life.

Thus we see four different Popes, in the sixteenth and seventeenth centuries, ordering the revelation of a sin of impurity, and forbidding it in cases of parricide. A woman confesses, or supposes in her confession to a Carmelite, that a Cordelier attempted to seduce her; the Carmelite must impeach the Cordelier. A fanatical assassin, believing that he shall serve God by killing his prince, consults his confessor on this case of conscience; the confessor is guilty of sacrilege if he save the life of his sovereign.

This horrible absurdity is one of the unhappy consequences of the continual opposition, which hath subsisted for so many ages, between the ecclesiastical and civil law. Mankind have in a thousand instances been suspended between the crimes of sacrilege and high-treason, and the distinctions of right and wrong have been buried in a chaos, from which they are not yet emerged.

Confession of sins hath been authorised in all times and in all nations. The ancients accused themselves in the mysteries of Orpheus, of Isis, of Ceres, of Samothrace. The Jews confessed their sins on the day of solemn expiation, and still continue the same practice. Each penitent chooses his confessor, who becomes his penitent in turn, and each receives from his companion thirty-nine lashes whilst he is repeating, three times, the formule of confession, which consists only in thirteen words, and which consequently must be general.

None of these confessions were particular, and consequently could never serve for a pretence to those secret consultations, under the shadow of which fanatical penitents think to sin with impunity; a pernicious practice, by which a salutary institution is corrupted. Confession, which was intended as a curb to iniquity, hath frequently, in times of confusion and seduction, become an incentive to wickedness. Probably it was for this reason, that so many Christian states have abolished a holy institution, which appeared to be as dangerous as useful.

OF FALSE MONEY.

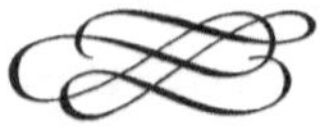

THE crime of coining false money is deemed high-treason in the second degree, and justly. To rob all the people is to be a traitor to the state. But it is asked whether a merchant who imports ingots of gold from America, and privately converts them into good money, be guilty of high-treason, and merit death? which is the punishment annexed to this crime in almost all countries. Nevertheless, he has robbed nobody; on the contrary, he has done service to the state by increasing the currency. But he hath defrauded the king of the small profit upon the coin. He hath indeed coined good money; but he hath led others into the temptation of coining bad. Yet death is a severe punishment. I knew a lawyer who was of opinion, that such a criminal should be condemned, as a useful hand, to work in the royal mint, with irons to his legs.

ON DOMESTIC THEFT.

IN countries where a trifling domestic theft, or breach of trust, is punished with death, is not the disproportioned punishment dangerous to society? Is it not even an encouragement to larceny? If, in this case, a master prosecutes his servant, and the unhappy wretch suffer death, the whole neighbourhood hold the master in abhorrence: they perceive that the law is contrary to nature, and consequently that it is a bad law.

What is the result? Masters, to avoid *opprobrium*, content themselves with discharging the thief, who afterwards steals from another, and gradually becomes familiar with dishonesty. The punishment being the same for a small theft as for a greater, he will naturally steal as much as he can, and at last will not scruple to turn assassin to prevent detection.

If, on the contrary, the punishment be proportioned to the crime; if those who are guilty of a

breach of trust be condemned to labour for the public, the master will not hesitate to bring the offender
to justice, and the crime will be less frequent: so true
it is, that rigorous laws are often productive of
crimes.

ON SUICIDE.

THE celebrated Du Verger de Hauranne, Abbè de St. Cyran, one of the founders of Port Royal, in the year 1608, wrote a treatise on suicide, which is become one of the scarcest books in Europe.

"The Decalogue," says that author, "forbids us to commit murder; in which precept self-murder seems no less to be understood, than the murder of another: if, therefore, there be cases in which it is lawful to kill another, there may be cases also wherein suicide may be allowed. But a man ought not to attempt his own life, till after having consulted his reason. Public authority, which is the representative of God, may dispose of our lives. The reason of man may also represent that of the Deity, it being a ray of the eternal light."

St. Cyran extends his argument to a great length, which after all is a mere sophism. But when he comes to exemplify, he is not quite so easily answered. "A man may kill himself," says he, "for the good of his prince, for the good of his country, or for the good of his parents."

It does not appear, that we could with justice condemn a Codrus, or a Curtius. What prince would dare to punish the family of a man who had sacrificed himself for his service? Or rather, is there any prince who would dare not to reward them. St. Thomas, before St. Cyran, said the same thing. But there was no need of either of Thomas, of Bonaventure, nor of Huranne, to inform us, that a man who dies for his country deserves our praise.

St. Cyran concludes, that it is lawful to do for one's own sake, that which is praise-worthy if done for another. The arguments of Plutarch, of Seneca, of Montaigne, and a hundred others, are well known. I do not pretend to apologise for an action which the laws have condemned; but I do not recollect, that either the Old or New Testament forbid a man to relinquish his life, when it is no longer supportable. By the Roman laws, suicide was not forbidden; on the contrary, in a law of Mark Antony, which was never repealed, we find it thus written: "If your brother or your father, being convicted of no crime, hath put himself to death, either to avoid pain, or being weary of life, or from despair or madness, his will shall nevertheless be valid, or his heirs inherit according to law."

Notwithstanding this humane law of our ancient masters, we ordain, that a stake shall be driven through the corps of the offender, and his memory becomes infamous. We do all in our power to dishonour his family. We punish a son for having lost a father, and a widow because she is deprived of her husband. We even confiscate the effects of the deceased, and rob the living of that which is justly their due. This custom, with many others, is derived from our canon law, which denies Christian burial to those who are guilty of suicide, concluding thence, that it is not lawful to inherit on earth from one who hath himself no inheritance in heaven. The cannon law assures us, that Judas committed a greater crime in hanging himself, than in betraying Jesus Christ.

ON A CERTAIN SPECIES OF MUTILATION.

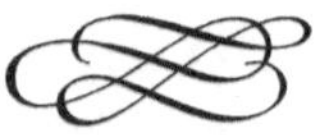

WE find, in the Pandect, a law of Adrian, which denounces death to the physicians who should make an eunuch, either by castration or by bruising the *testes*. By the same law, the possessions of those who suffered castration were confiscated. Origen ought certainly to have been punished, who submitted to this operation, from the rigid interpretation of that passage in St. Matthew, which says, *There be eunuchs, which have made themselves eunuchs for the kingdom of heaven's sake.*

Things changed in the reigns of succeeding emperors, who adopted the luxury of Asia; especially in the lower empire of Constantinople, where eunuchs became patriarchs and generals of armies.

In these our own times, it is the custom at Rome to castrate young children, to render them worthy of being musicians to his Holiness; so that *Castrato* and *Musico del Papa* are synonimous. It is not long since you might have seen at Naples, written in great letters over the doors of certain barbers, *Qui si castrano mar avigliosamente i puti:* here boys are castrated in the best manner.

ON CONFISCATION.

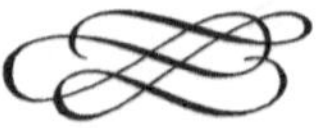

IT is a maxim received at the bar, that *he who forfeits his life forfeits his effects;* a maxim which prevails in those countries where custom serves instead of law. So that, as we have already observed, the children of one who puts an end to his own life, are condemned to perish with hunger, equally with those of an assassin. Thus, in every case, a whole family is punished for the crime of an individual. Thus when the father of a family is condemned to the gallies for life, by an arbitrary sentence, whether it be for having harboured a preacher, or for hearing his sermon in a cavern or a desert, his wife and children are reduced to beg their bread.

That law which consists in depriving an orphan of support, and in giving to one man the possessions of another, was unknown in the times of the Roman republic. It was first introduced by Sylla, in his proscriptions, whose example one would scarce have thought worthy imitation. Nor indeed was this law adopted by Cesar, by Trajan, or by Antoninus, whose name is still pronounced with respect by all nations; and under Justinian, confiscation took place only in case of high-treason.

It seems that, in the times of feudal anarchy, princes and lords not being very rich, sought to increase their revenue by the condemnation of their subjects. Their laws being arbitrary, and the Roman jurisprudence unknown, customs either cruel or ridiculous prevailed. But now that the power of princes is founded on immense and certain revenues, there can be no need to swell their treasuries with the inconsiderable wreck of an unfortunate family.

In countries where the Roman law is established, confiscation is not admitted, except within the jurisdiction of the parliament of Toulouse. It was formerly the law at Calais, but was abolished by the English, whilst that city was in their possession. It is strange, that the inhabitants of the capital should be subject to a severer law than the people in the country: but laws, like the cottages in a village, were generally established by accident, and without attention to the regularity of a general plan.

Who would believe that, in the year 1673, in the most brilliant period of the kingdom of France, the advocate-general, Omer Talon, did in full parliament express himself, on the subject of a young lady named Canillac, in the following words:

"God says, in the 13th chapter of Deuteronomy, If thou comest into a city where idolatry reigneth, thou shalt surely smite the inhabitants of that city with the edge of the sword, destroying it utterly and all that is therein. And thou shalt gather all the spoil thereof into the midst of the street, and shalt burn with fire the city, and all the spoil thereof, for the Lord thy God; and it shall be an heap for ever; and there shall cleave nought of the cursed thing to thine hand."

"In like manner, in the crime of high-treason, the children were deprived of their inheritance, which became forfeited to the king. Naboth being prosecuted *quia maledixerat regi,* king Ahab took possession of his effects. David being informed that Mephibosheth had rebelled, gave all his possessions to Ziba who brought him the news: *tua sint omnia quæ fuerunt Mephibosheth.* "

The question in dispute was, who should inherit the paternal estate of Mlle. de Canillac, which having been confiscated, was abandoned by the king to a lord of the treasury, and afterwards bequeathed by him to the testatrix. In this cause concerning a girl of Auvergne it was, that an advocate-general referred to Ahab, king of a part of Palestine, who confiscated the vineyard of Naboth, after assassinating the owner with the sword of justice: an action so abominable as to have passed into a proverb, intended to inspire mankind with detestation for such acts of tyranny. There was certainly no analogy between the vineyard of Naboth and the inheritance of Mlle. de Canillac; nor hath the murder and confiscation of the possessions of Mephibosheth, the grandson of Saul, and son of Jonathan, the friend and protector of David, the least affinity with the will of this lady.

It was with such pedantry, with such foolish quotations foreign to the subject, with such ignorance of the first principles of human nature, with such prejudices ill conceived and ill applied, that laws have been explained and executed, by men who acquired reputation in their sphere. I leave to the reader that, which to tell him were superfluous.

ON CRIMINAL PROCEDURE, AND OTHER FORMS.

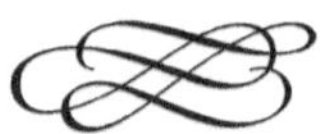

I F, in France, it should ever happen that the laws of humanity soften some of our rigorous customs, without facilitating the commission of crimes, we may hope for reformation in those legal proceedings, wherein our legislators seem to have been influenced by too much severity. Our criminal procedure appears in many instances to point only at the destruction of the accused. It is the only law which is uniform throughout the whole kingdom; a law which ought certainly to be no less favourable to the innocent, than terrible to the guilty.

In England a man may recover damages for false imprisonment. In France, on the contrary, an innocent person, who has had the misfortune to be thrown into a dungeon and tortured almost to death, has no consolation, no damages to hope for, no action against any one; and to add to his misfortune, he has for ever lost his reputation. Why? Because his joints have been dislocated; a circumstance which ought rather to inspire compassion and respect. The discovery of crimes, say they, requires severity: it is a war of human justice against iniquity. But there is generosity and compassion even in war. The brave are ever compassionate; and shall the law delight in barbarity?

Let us compare the criminal procedure of the Romans with ours. With them, the evidence were heard publicly in presence of the accused, who might answer or interrogate them, or employ counsel. This procedure was open and noble; it breathed Roman magnanimity.

With us, all is conducted in secret. A single judge, only attended by his clerk, hears each witness separately. This custom, established by Francis I. was confirmed by the commissioners who were employed to digest the ordinance of Lewis XIV. in 1670; which confirmation was entirely owing to a mistake. They imagined, in reading the code *de Testibus*, that the words *testes intrare judicii secretum,* signified that the witnesses were examined in private; but *secretum* means here the chamber of the judge. *Intrare secretum,* if intended to signify private interrogation, would be false Latin. This part of our law therefore is founded on a solecism.

The evidence in these cases are commonly the dregs of the people, whom the judge may, in such private examination, make say whatever he pleases. They are examined a second time, but still privately; and if, after this re-examination, they retract from their deposition, or vary in any material circumstance, they are punished as false evidence. So that if a simple honest fellow, recollecting that he has said too much, that he misunderstood the judge, or the judge him, revoke his deposition from a principle of justice, he is punished as a reprobate. The natural consequence of this is, that men will confirm a false testimony rather than expose themselves, for their honesty, to certain punishment.

The law seems to oblige the magistrate to be the enemy of the accused, rather than his judge; it being left in the power of the magistrate to confront the evidence with the accused, or not, as he shall think proper. Amazing! that so necessary a part of the procedure should be left undetermined.

A man being suspected of a crime, knowing that he is denied the benefit of counsel, flies his country; a step to which he is encouraged by every maxim of the law. But he may be condemned in his absence, whether the crime be proved or not. Strange laws! If a man be charged with owing a sum of money, before he can be condemned to pay the demand, it is required that the debt be proved; but if his life be in question, he may be condemned, by default, without any proof of the crime. Is money then of more importance than life? O ye judges and legislators! Consult the pious Antoninus, and the good Trajan: they suffered not the absent to be condemned.

Do your laws then allow the privilege of counsel to an extortioner, or a fraudulent bankrupt, and refuse it to one who may possibly be a very honest and honourable man? If there ever were an instance of innocence being justified by means of counsel, the law, which deprives the accused of that benefit, is evidently unjust.

The parliament of Toulouse hath a very singular custom relative to the validity of evidence. In other places demi-proofs are admitted, which is a palpable absurdity, there being no such thing as demi-truth; but at Toulouse they admit of quarters and eighths of a proof. For instance, an hearsay may be considered as a quarter, and another hearsay, more vague than the former, as an eighth: so that eight hearsays, which in fact are no other than an echo of a groundless report, constitute a full proof. Upon this principle it was, that poor Calas was condemned to the *wheel*.

THE IDEA OF REFORMATION.

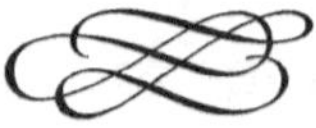

MAGISTRATES are in themselves so respectable, that the inhabitants of the only country in which they are venal, sincerely pray to be delivered from this custom: they wish that the civilian may by his merit establish that justice, which in his writings he hath so nobly defended. We may then possibly hope to see a regular and uniform system of laws.

Shall the law of the provinces be always at variance with the law in the capital? Shall a man be right in Britanny, and wrong in Languedoc? Nay, there are as many laws as there are towns; and, even in the same parliament, the maxims of one chamber are not the maxims of another.

What astonishing contrariety in the laws of one kingdom! In Paris, a man who has been an inhabitant during one year and a day, is reputed a citizen. In *Franche-Comte,* a freeman who, during a year and a day, inhabits a house in mortmain, becomes a slave; his collateral heirs are excluded from inheriting his foreign acquisitions, and even his children are deprived of their inheritance, if they have been a year absent from the house in which the father died. This province is called *Franche,* but where is their freedom?

Were we to attempt to draw a line between civil authority and ecclesiastical customs, what endless disputes would ensue? In short, to what side soever we turn our eyes, we are presented with a confused scene of contradictions, uncertainty, hardships, and arbitrary power. In the present age, we seem universally aiming at perfection; let us not therefore neglect to perfect the laws, on which our lives and fortunes depend.

BECCARIA, bĕk'kȧ-rḗ'ȧ, Cesare Bonesano, Marquis of (1735-93). An Italian economist and jurist, born in Milan. The opinions of the French encyclopædists, as well as those of Montesquieu, had the greatest influence on the development of his thought. He wrote on the currency and other economic subjects, but his greatest work was his *Trattato dei delitti e delle pene* (Treatise on Crimes and Punishments), first published in 1764, in which he argues against capital punishment, and which established his fame as the originator of more humane methods in dealing with criminals. The work was extremely popular, passing through six editions within eighteen months, and was translated into many European languages. Kent unfairly accuses the author of an affected humanity, but did expose the invalidity of some of the arguments brought forward. Beccaria was among the first to advocate the beneficial influence of education in lessening crime. In 1768 Beccaria was appointed professor of public law and economy at Milan, and achieved great success as a lecturer. His lectures are published in the Italian collection, *Scrittori classici italiani*, Vols. XI. and XII., where also a biographical sketch will be found. A translation of his essay on "Crimes and Punishments" is included in J. A. Farrar's *Crimes and Punishments* (New York, 1872; London, 1880).

In *The New International Encyclopædia* , 1905

www.ingramcontent.com/pod-product-compliance
Lightning Source LLC
LaVergne TN
LVHW091437210726
843527LV00033B/513